Haynes

Cat

Manual

First published in September 2009

British Library Cataloguing in Publication Data
A catalogue record for this book is available from the British Library

ISBN 978 1 84425 675 4

Library of Congress control no. 2009923208

Published by Haynes Publishing,
Sparkford, Yeovil, Somerset BA22 7JJ, UK
Tel: 01963 442030 Fax: 01963 440001
Int. tel: +44 1963 442030 Int. fax: +44 1963 440001
E-mail: sales@haynes.co.uk
Website: www.haynes.co.uk

Haynes North America Inc.
861 Lawrence Drive, Newbury Park,
California 91320, USA

Printed and bound in the UK

Credits

Author:	**Claire Bessant**
Project Manager:	**Louise McIntyre**
Copy editor:	**Ian Heath**
Page design:	**James Robertson**
Index:	**Elisabeth Pickard**

Photography:

top = t, bottom = b, r = right
Alamy: 67 (Ocicat), 68 (Singapura), 70 (Manx, Savannah), 139
Feline Advisory Bureau: 83(r), 96 (x4), 102(b), 129 (Cress Green Cattery), 130 (Little Happy Cattery), 131(Minety Cattery)
Warren Photographic: 4 (x2), 6, 8(b), 10, 12, 18(b), 26, 27(b), 29(b), 30, 44, 52(t), 53(b), 54(b), 55(b), 61(b), 65 (Birman, Turkish Van), 66(t), 67 (Korat, Egyptian Mau), 68 (Exotic, Snowshoe), 133(t)
Page 23, skull xray, Samantha Taylor and Frances Barr, University of Bristol
Page 138 , fence system - Katzecure Ltd
page 16, illustration - Matthew Marke
All other images from istockphoto.com

Haynes

Cat
Manual

The complete step-by-step guide to understanding and caring for your cat

Claire Bessant

CONTENTS

INTRODUCTION

So what?

I've written many books on cats and I work on a daily basis with cat vets, behaviourists, breeders, cattery owners, people involved with the rescue or feral cats and, of course, cat owners. There's a wealth of information around on cats, but not all of it is reliable. However, I hope that over the years I've gleaned sufficient wisdom from the exceptional people around me, and from dealing with queries and problems raised by cat owners and carers, to provide not only some sound common-sense care advice but also useful insights into the lives of these fantastic animals.

In this book I'm not going to follow the usual simple approach of plodding through breeds or behaviour. Instead I'm going to take what we know about the cat and how it interacts with its environment and integrate that into its

relationship with us, how we can make it feel happy and how we can keep it healthy.

What most people want is to have the best relationship it's possible to have with their cat for the longest time. There are things that we can do as owners to maximise this. From choosing the right cat for our situation in the first place, to giving it a home where it can feel safe and secure and keeping it healthy, we have to realise that we have a significant effect on how our cats live. So if we can gain an insight into how cats see the world and what's important to them, then we can understand how any changes we make to their environment and their care will affect them.

I suppose what I want to present is a sort of 'so what?' approach. Looking at the perfect hunting machine that evolution has produced and how it uses all of its skills might be interesting, but what does it have to do with how cats live with us? My aim is to present you with what we know, what

we guess and what we don't know, and then examine how that affects the way cats live closely with humans.

I will look at breeds, but in the context of health rather than what looks pretty. I'll also look at the way we want to live with our cats and how they might prefer to be kept; and, of course, at what we can understand about our individual pets from the way they behave.

The pet of the future

Why choose a cat as a pet? That question doesn't arise for some people. To ailurophiles, or real cat-lovers, who just adore everything about this little feline – its shape, its colour, its temperament and all of its foibles – it can do no wrong. Quite often these people are women, quite often they're creative folk who admire the independent spirit of the cat and its beauty.

Of course, the cat is also a great family pet, happy to sit with young or old, agile or disabled – a warm lap can belong to anyone. Without the need to be walked or physically controlled, the cat works well as a pet for all. Men too, these days, are allowed to say that they enjoy the challenge of a cat; those who let themselves get to know and appreciate a cat, rather than trying to control it like a dog, will be as flattered as anyone else that this creature, which can live as well in the wild as it can with us, has chosen to spend time with them.

These days there are far more restrictions on our keeping

Clever and beautiful . . . but what makes a cat happy?

pets. Dogs need to be controlled and walked, we can't leave them alone all day when we work, and they need to be cleared up after if we walk them outside. There's considerable legislation concerning them, both for our physical safety and regarding cleaning up their waste. Indeed, they can even be dangerous to people or to other dogs, and occasionally things do go wrong. Cats too might scratch or bite, but they're rarely as dangerous as dogs or as difficult to keep.

Cats are good pets for single people – a warm welcome to come home to without having the guilt of having to leave an animal on its own all day, as cats often like to be alone. Cats are also great with families and enjoy sleeping on various different beds and getting the attention of adults and children alike.

Being happy either to go out into the great outdoors or to use a litter tray indoors, cats are flexible too. Large house or flat, they use all of the space available, vertical as well as horizontal, and are much more 'nose-friendly' than dogs – they're much less smelly and keep themselves clean and tidy.

You can get a kitten or an adult cat, a neutered male or female, a tabby or a black-and-white, show-ready beautiful or rather battered – all can make brilliant companions and trouble-free pets. They can live for a long time and often in great health; they're affectionate, fun and beautiful to watch. All in all, you really can't beat a cat.

Cats and children

There are many myths regarding cats and babies or young children. Cats actually make great pets for kids, as long as the children are taught from an early age to respect them, and the proper way to approach and handle them.

Cats and babies

Every pregnant mother-to-be worries about anything that might prove a potential threat to a new baby. Indeed, many pregnant women are advised to get rid of their cat before the baby is born. This is such a shame, because with the correct care and by taking a sensible approach cats can actually be great company for a new mother who has to do a great deal of sitting still to feed the baby. Some cats really enjoy the extra time spent sitting and purring next to mum and baby, and soon accept the presence of a new addition to the family as normal, or even a bonus. However, sensible precautions that should be taken are:

- Keep the cat out of the baby's room and cot.
- If you leave the baby asleep in a pram put a cat net over the top to prevent the cat sitting in it.
- Wash your hands after handling the cat.

Cats and toddlers

The phase during which a new baby is entirely helpless only lasts for a short time. Thereafter you have to start protecting the cat from the baby as it becomes more mobile and prone to grabbing and pulling. Even when a baby is very young you can take his or her hand and gently stroke the cat to show how it should be done, stopping if the cat becomes worried.

This will establish the right pattern for subsequent interaction with the cat. Always emphasise being gentle and quiet, and discourage grabbing at the cat. Never let a baby or child pull a cat's tail or any other part!

Reward both the baby or toddler and the cat for quiet interaction but never leave them together unattended. As the baby becomes a toddler make sure that the cat can escape to high places in order to get some peace and quiet.

Most cats take all of this in their stride and soon learn to remove themselves from the situation if it all gets a little too noisy, exciting or dangerous. Of course, cats, like people, have different personalities and more nervous felines may need more time to adapt or more places to escape to. Alternatively, if you have a rather feisty cat then you may need to be a little more vigilant to prevent your child from being rough when playing with it, as the cat may react by scratching or biting.

Remember that crawling babies and toddlers may find the cat litter tray and its content rather fascinating and that the cat may be put off using it if grabbed by a child every time it goes there.

Small children

If you get a new cat or kitten when your children are small, take time to explain to them that it's not a toy, that it's vulnerable and that it's likely to be scared of them at first. Explain that shouting, loud noises and sudden movements will be frightening. Giving them the responsibility of trying to be kind and quiet with the cat will encourage them – don't just wait until a child has grabbed the cat and then shout at them for doing it wrong. Lead by example and teach your children how to hold the cat properly (see below).

If you stay calm, be sensible and teach your children to be respectful and gentle, then cats and kids can have a great relationship. The good thing about cats is that they're long-lived and can grow up alongside a baby and form a bond that can last for many years.

Making introductions: handling a cat

If you have a new kitten or cat, sit the children on the floor and let the animal investigate them. Give the kids a small treat to offer the cat, to encourage interaction. If the cat is happy to be touched encourage the kids to stroke its head and along its back gently. If the cat walks away don't let the children chase it, but quietly encourage it to come back.

When it comes to picking up the cat, make sure the child is strong enough if the cat is full-grown. Ideally the first time should be when the child is sitting, perhaps on the settee, and the cat is on it too. Just lift the cat gently on to the child's lap and then by stroking the cat encourage it to sit down and stay. Again, encourage rather than force interaction.

Right: Teaching a gentle approach from the beginning makes interaction enjoyable for all parties.

When it comes to lifting a cat from the ground, this should be done by placing one hand under its chest and scooping it up, placing the other hand under its bottom to support its weight. Hold it gently against your chest to make it feel safe – if it feels insecure it may well panic and struggle. Demonstrate how to do this before letting your children try. When your child has picked the cat up, encourage them to talk to it softly, and to put it down gently should it try to get away.

A kitten is obviously more fragile than a full-grown cat and children should do their initial lifting over a soft surface to avoid it being injured should it leap from their arms. Children also need to understand that kittens need time to sleep and should be given a chance to do this. If several children are vying for the kitten's attentions then it may not get a chance to sleep while they take turns to pick it up and hug it.

Also explain some basic feline body language – the warning signs that should be watched out for. A swishing tail, for instance, usually means the cat feels threatened and irritated by the attention it's getting. Flattened ears, struggling to get away, hissing, etc, are all quite extreme signals that a cat isn't happy, and the children should back off. They also need to understand that the cat may be reactive for some time afterwards and need time to calm down, and will need to be approached differently in the future.

FROM A CAT'S PERSPECTIVE

Think cat

If cats were humans they'd be the kind of people that we'd feel privileged to be around. They're rather proud, definitely good-looking, they don't try too hard and they won't pretend to like you if they don't. If they give you attention you feel that the sun is shining on you; they're also great for cuddles. Granted they won't save you from a burning building or make you a cup of tea; it's more like having grace and favour bestowed upon us – it makes us *feel* good.

The cat family is arguably the most beautiful group of species – from coat texture and colours to body form, size and colour of eye and, of course, that wonderful purr. To have a mini-version of a tiger as a pet should not be taken for granted.

In this section I want to look at how cats look at us and the way we live, to enable us to see things from a different perspective so that we understand why certain things either feel good to a cat or frighten it, why they make it feel secure or why they make it want to leave home.

What's a cat for?

Forget the word 'pet' for a moment. Take people out of the equation and look at the cat in its own world without interference. What does it need to do?

Like all of us, the cat must have food and water in order to survive and needs to reproduce in order to keep the species going. It may not be aware that its need to procreate is for the good of the species, or that its instinctive territoriality is there to keep other cats away so that it can survive on the prey within its own 'patch'; but its actions will be shaped by these drives.

Let's look at survival first, survival of the cat itself rather than the species.

The cat is a little animal but it's chock-full of fantastic talents and 'gadgets' to help it to catch prey. This prey consists most often those little mammals with lightning-fast reactions that scurry around in the undergrowth, often as it's getting dark. Cats may also try to catch birds, which have that extra dimension in which to escape, making the task even more difficult. Some brave cats even catch rats (a full-grown rat fighting for its life is a serious adversary, and could cause great damage to a cat). Others catch larger prey still, such as baby rabbits (or almost fully grown ones), pheasants, pigeons, etc, and may even try to drag them in through the cat flap.

So, how do you get anywhere near one of these prey creatures, which have great hearing and can scamper away in seconds? You have to be able to hunt in the dark, to use sound to pinpoint your prey, be able to get close enough to rush in and grab it before it knows you're there and kill it quickly before it bites you or wriggles away. With such

A cat's behaviour is shaped by its instinctive survival drives – such as hunting.

small prey you'll need to eat about ten a day, and every hunt will certainly not be successful. So you need to be good. *Very* good.

At the same time you'll need to defend your area from other cats so that they don't eat the prey on it, in order to ensure there's enough food for you to survive on; and, occasionally, you'll need to meet another cat in order to mate and produce kittens. Females will then need to hunt even more efficiently in order to feed the kittens and raise them, and then teach them how to hunt and survive before going on to repeat the whole process again during the next breeding season. If you're male you'll need to be fit enough to fight off other toms for territory and, of course, for females, in order to mate successfully.

Although you're a hunter and thus feared by the many small creatures that you hunt, you're also a relatively small creature and could become prey yourself. So, while hunting and defending your territory against your own species, you also need to make sure you're not in danger.

What does the world look like to a cat?

If you've ever looked after a human toddler you'll know that these bundles of energy can get themselves into all sorts of trouble by touching and eating just about everything they come across. The best way to prepare and to remove dangers is to actually get down to toddler-level and look around – it's amazing how different the world looks and what can be pulled over, found on the carpet or poked with a tiny finger. The same goes for a cat. Seeing a room from knee-height really changes your perspective and puts you in the right mind-frame to think like a cat.

The cat has some amazing talents in terms of its ability to jump and balance, and this gives it access to areas above it. It can be confident of its ability to jump up as well as to run away, giving it a much larger world to occupy than, for example, a dog.

Think about the cat in the wild – what does it need to be able to do? Its Number One priority is to hunt in order to survive. We all know how easy it is to get cats to chase a moving object. That's because they're programmed to react to small objects moving away from them and can respond quickly to opportunities without having to waste time thinking about what to do – it's instinctive.

They also have large numbers of light sensitive cells at

Right: The cat's eye is a highly sophisticated tool necessary for hunting successfully.

Why can't cats resist playing with a moving object?

In order to be an excellent hunter and to survive, a cat has to be able to react extremely quickly to catch a potential meal. It's equipped with extra movement sensors in its eyes so that it's very sensitive to small things moving away from it, and this movement triggers an automatic response which puts the cat into hunt mode. To be a good hunter you can't afford to spend a great deal of time thinking – your reaction needs to be automatic. We exploit this reaction when we play with cats, triggering them into hunt or play mode. They just can't resist!

the back of the eye that can pick up light at a much lower level than we can. This, in addition to the special layer of cells which reflect light at the back of the eye (we can see this when the cat's eyes take on a greenish glow when we use a camera flash to photograph them) mean that cats can see in very low light – essential if you're out and about hunting at dawn and dusk. Cats are what are known as crepuscular hunters, meaning active in the twilight at dawn and dusk, when their prey is moving about.

This is also the reason why many pet cats are up and about early, jumping on to the bed to prod us into action, to let them out or feed them – their natural rhythms mean they're active at this time. While cats can't see in the absolute dark, the number of hours each day when they can see well enough to move around easily is much greater than for us.

The cat has very large eyes proportionally to its head size, and the area which lets light in to hit the light sensitive cells at the back can be adjusted enormously – the pupil can open almost as wide as the whole eye (making the eye look black) or can close to a thin slit so that almost all of the eye is the colour of the pupil. When you have such a sensitive organ, that can maximise the visual information reaching the optic nerve and the brain, you also need to be able to protect it: too much light getting in could even damage the eye, so the beautifully coloured pupil can shut right down and let just a tiny fraction through.

Cats have additional protection for their eyes in the form of a third eyelid, which can be deployed rapidly when needed. It's officially called the nictitating membrane and most of the time it's tucked away and you won't see it at all. However, if your cat is unwell or has an eye problem

you may well notice that it has what looks like a thin film of tissue or membrane over the lower inside corner of its eye.

What about colours – does a cat see in colour? The question should probably be 'does a cat *need* to see in colour?' As has been mentioned, cats are most active at dawn and dusk. Imagine being out at that time of day – it's a very weird time for us and it can be very difficult to distinguish and differentiate objects. Everything loses its colour and takes on a greyish hue. It's a time when we want people walking along the road to wear something white or reflective so that we don't accidentally drive into them. It's thought that cats don't see strong colours but rather muted hues of blue and green, with reds and oranges looking grey. They hunt in the twilight and their prey is grey or brown, so colour isn't that important. What's of value is being able to see in this reduced visibility and notice movement. However, it's possible that other cat species that hunt more colourful prey have evolved to see brighter colours.

How all of this comes together in the hunt is outlined on page 21.

What does the world sound like to a cat?

Once again we need to think about function in order to understand the importance of hearing to a cat, and how its ears are designed to maximise this.

Left: Cats are alert to tiny movements.

Below: The cat's ears act like mobile satellite dishes, scanning the surroundings to pick up signs of prey or danger.

Left: The cat probably sees the world in muted colours.

Above: The cat's sensitive pads can pick up vibrations, adding to the array of information coming into its brain.

Cats have fantastic ears, perched on the top of the head, with a great swivel action that enables them to collect sound by acting like satellite dishes. If a small creature is in the undergrowth and can't be seen then the cat needs to be able to home in on it simply using sound, so its hearing system needs to be ultra-sensitive to be able to pick up the very high-pitched squeaks and rustles made by small mammals. It then needs to be able to direct the cat to the source of the sound so that it can get close enough to pounce. From the tender age of just four weeks kittens can use this hearing system to pinpoint prey as accurately as an adult, showing just how quickly kittens have to grow up and start learning to hunt.

Cats are more sensitive than dogs to high-pitched sounds – in fact they have a very wide range of sensitivity, from 30 Hertz to 50,000 Hertz, which allows them to hear sounds almost as low as humans can to those way beyond human hearing. Indeed, the only animals with a wider range are the horse and the porpoise. Remember, the cat has got to eavesdrop on its prey, to be able to hear the chatter and rustling as they go about their daily lives.

When we talk to our cats we often use a higher-pitched voice, and perhaps this is instinctive because we've noticed that our cats react to this range rather than lower human sounds, which they may not be able to hear so well.

As with everything else about this compact little hunter, its hearing works brilliantly. The ears, which can swivel independently and are also often used to show emotions, can 'catch' sound and amplify and channel it down into the inner ear, the difference between the sounds that reach each ear allowing the cat to pinpoint their source. Cats can distinguish between sound sources that are 8cm (3in) apart from a distance of 2m (6ft), or 40cm (15in) apart 20m (60 ft) away. In this way a cat can slowly creep towards

potential prey, picking up information all the time as it homes in accurately for that final pounce.

So the world is a pretty noisy place for a cat. Imagine being able to just sit there and swivel your ears, picking up tiny sounds all around. Even when the cat is doing that 'sitting and dozing with eyes half shut' thing, its ears are still turning like radar dishes, monitoring its surroundings.

The pads of a cat's feet are also highly sensitive, particularly the front ones (some cats use their front paws in a very hand-like way and are very dextrous). Not only do these pads cushion the cat's walk, they're also sensitive organs. A cat is said to be able to 'hear' with its feet because the pads are so sensitive to vibration. Special pressure receptors may detect vibrations in the ground caused by rodents moving around, as well as giving the cat information about the texture and temperature of the ground it's walking over.

What does the world smell and taste like to a cat?

While we can imagine ourselves down in the grass listening to the movement and squeaking of small rodents, and perhaps we can even blur our eyes and imagine seeing in muted colours and in the dark, I suspect that the world of scent that the cat inhabits is beyond our imagination. In our vision-orientated lives smell probably comes at the bottom of our list of senses. And just as our sense of taste is affected if we can't smell well, the cat's senses of smell and taste are equally linked. Indeed, the combination results in something much more amazing.

What we do know is that behind that tiny nose the cat has an area lined with special cells which, if it was laid flat, would be the size of a small handkerchief. Not surprisingly, this is twice the size of the human equivalent, but not quite as large as in a dog's nose. Of course, a cat doesn't hunt using its sense of smell like a dog does. For cats, smell is about communication and feeding.

A cat walking through a garden or into a room can tell all sorts of things about who's been there, when other cats have left marks and scent signals. If the signals were coloured there'd be smudges and bright spots, mists and fading areas, and to a cat this scent-picture is as strong as our visual one.

But the sensitivity of a cat's sense of smell isn't the end of the story. To enable them to gain even more information about the scent messages that have been left for them, cats use a special organ that's located just above the roof of the mouth. By raising its lips, sucking in and pressing its tongue against the roof of its mouth the cat can push air into this little cigar-shaped sac (called Jacobson's organ), allowing it to really concentrate the scent molecules and what could be described as 'smell/taste' them, and by this process get much more information than it could by doing just one or the other. There's a very characteristic facial expression that accompanies this behaviour, known as the flehmen response. The cat often does this with scents that have reproductive messages in them – male cats will do it when they sniff the urine of female cats in season.

Taste

Once again we have to arrest our own expectations of taste when we try to imagine what a cat experiences when it eats or smells food. Just about everything cats eat in the wild is meat-based. Indeed, cats have to eat meat in order to acquire the nutrients they need, being what's known as obligate carnivores.

How animals perceive 'taste' – what they experience when the receptors associated with certain chemicals are activated – is almost impossible to tell. Like humans, the cat has a tongue covered with small lumps called papillae, a cluster of taste buds that react to different components of the cat's diet. The saliva dissolves some of the food and the chemicals activate the taste buds. It's thought that, like us, cats can distinguish between sour, bitter and salty tastes. However, they don't seem to be able to taste what we call 'sweet'. This would make sense, as sugar mice aren't very abundant in the big wide world, so why develop a receptor

Above: The cat's world of scent may be very difficult for us to imagine.

Below: An extra tool! Cats have help in their detection of smell and taste. The Jacobson's organ is found in the roof of the mouth.

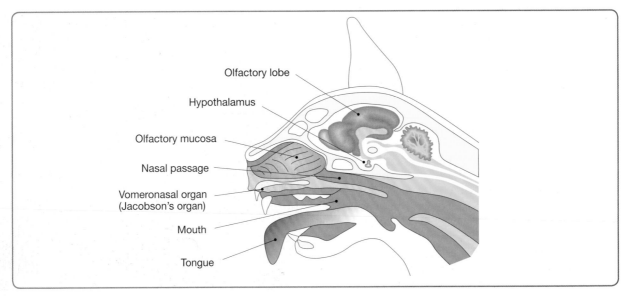

- Olfactory lobe
- Hypothalamus
- Olfactory mucosa
- Nasal passage
- Vomeronasal organ (Jacobson's organ)
- Mouth
- Tongue

for something you're unlikely to come across? We developed our liking for sweet things because, as we were evolving, sweet things containing energy-giving sugar were few and far between – just honey and a few plants – and we were programmed to seek them out. However, cats didn't have or need this source of energy. Instead they evolved to be meat specialists, and actually lost some of the pathways our bodies have that allow us to use the nutrients available from other food that we could scavenge or gather.

Maybe a mouse tastes very different to a rat, or a bird, or a shrew, who knows? Cats are probably experts on the different tastes of fat or protein – their liking for dairy products such as milk, cream and cheese may show that they like a high fat content or the texture of a food. Perhaps some of the chemicals they contain give cats the same pleasurable response that we get from chocolate and sweet foods.

Given a choice, it's thought that cats will usually choose a food that has a high meat fat content, a strong smell, a mixture of soft and crispy textures and is served at about body temperature. They enjoy variety in their diet and will often try a new food or flavour in preference to one they're more used to – unless they're feeling under threat or stress, when they're more lively to choose something they're familiar with – perhaps our equivalent of 'comfort' food.

What does the world feel like to a cat?

A cat is a very sensual creature – it is very sensitive to touch and controls its beautiful body gracefully and sensitively. But how does it place itself within its environment? How does it 'feel' the world around it?

Think of a dog and then think of a cat, and how differently they move and interact within their world. The difference between the barging, clumsy dog and the delicate cat is all down to how sensitive they are. Like humans and dogs, cats have pressure- and touch-sensitive receptors on their skin. These can distinguish between sensations such as stroking, tickling or brushing. Temperature and pain receptors also give the cat information about how its environment is impacting upon it. However, because cats have to move carefully and silently through the world around them in dark conditions, they have to be really 'tuned in' to what's all around them. It's not a case of bashing through, but rather of tiptoeing, twisting and avoiding, stepping quietly and waiting, being highly sensitive to everything around it.

A cat's coat and whiskers are very important in 'feeling' its surroundings. How can you enhance your sensitivity to

Below: Taking stock of its environment, the cat will tiptoe rather than barge through.

what's happening around you, to tell you if you're touching vegetation, whether there's a breeze, if there's an obstacle nearby, or what's underfoot, and whether it's likely to make a noise and give you away or reassure you that everything's safe? Such things are vital to a cat's survival. One way to do it is to sense even the slightest brush against an obstacle, or even the air that's moving around it. This is where the cat's coat comes into play. All over it are 'guard hairs', specialised thickened hairs that penetrate more deeply into the skin than others and have many nerves at their roots. These special hairs (and whiskers are included in this category) act like levers, and any movement they make is amplified so that the cat is aware of it. So with this sensitive 'force field' around it the cat can feel its way around in the dark, in narrow spaces, or in the undergrowth when it needs to close its vulnerable eyes to make sure they're not injured.

The whiskers themselves extend to about double the width of the face (about body width), and other hair over

the eyes, chin and cheeks make the head even more sensitive than the body. Later we'll see how the whiskers are also vital in hunting and killing prey.

This is why cats seem to be able to duck away from you if you try to stroke them with a wet hand, or twitch as something seems to almost but not quite touch them. They're highly aware of the world around them and their suppleness and lightness of movement enable them to be graceful and balanced.

Added to this are the highly sensitive pads under their paws, which are soft and compliant in comparison to the harsh, hard, scratchy pads of a dog's feet. As has been mentioned, these

allow a cat to almost 'hear' with its feet, picking up movement and vibrations and giving the cat yet more information.

Our pet cats have evolved from desert-living ancestors and their bodies have adaptations that enable them to thrive in heat. Perhaps this is why cats aren't so sensitive to heat as we humans are – you'll have seen your own cat sitting on the radiator, boiler or Rayburn, oblivious to the heat. The nose and upper lip, however, are particularly sensitive to temperature, probably so that as kittens they could follow the route to the warmest spot – under their mother's belly to suck milk.

Making the most of its talents

We've seen how the cat can use its senses of sight and smell to notice and pinpoint prey and how its sensitivity to touch allows it to move with such grace and success through its environment. But a cat needs more than this to get itself to its prey quickly and then to catch and kill it. What other advantages does this top-of-the-food-chain predator have over other similar-sized animals that don't need to hunt to stay alive?

What makes a cat so graceful and fluid in its movements? To begin with, the cat's skeleton

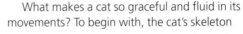

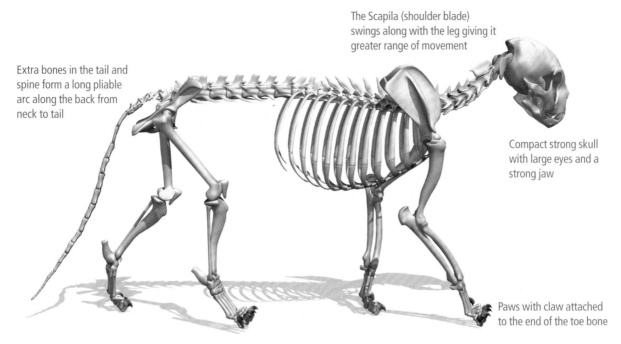

Extra bones in the tail and spine form a long pliable arc along the back from neck to tail

The Scapila (shoulder blade) swings along with the leg giving it greater range of movement

Compact strong skull with large eyes and a strong jaw

Paws with claw attached to the end of the toe bone

The small compact body of the cat is strong, flexible and finely controlled.

and muscles are designed to give it great flexibility, agility and speed of movement. If you wanted to design a vehicle to do what the cat does then everything would have to be made of high-quality components, rounded and streamlined, yet flexible and tough. Like all mammals, the cat's body is made of up muscles linked to the bone system. The most powerful are in its hindquarters, to give it the strength to pounce, and in its jaws, to help it kill its prey.

The feline adaptations that help it to be so agile include a 'floating' collarbone. This isn't actually attached to the shoulder joint, as it is in humans, but instead sits unattached in the muscle and allows the shoulders to move with little restriction, to get it into small places or put its feet directly in front of each other if it has to balance along a narrow fence.

Watch your cat hunting. When it stalks its prey its shoulder blades rise and fall as it steps forward; at the same time the head and spine remain motionless, eyes and ears fixed on its

Do cats really fall on their feet?

One of the cat's unique characteristics is its ability to land on its feet after a fall, known as its 'righting reflex'. While cats don't land safely after every fall or from any height (many are injured), they do nevertheless enjoy a remarkable ability to save themselves by turning around in midair and landing on all fours.

As a cat falls an automatic response mode is triggered that enables it to flip over. In less than one tenth of a second, information from its eyes and the balance sensory organs in its ears trigger a sequence of movements that first turn the cat so that its head is horizontal and upright, and then bring round the front part of its body. Nerves in the spine cause the back end of the body to follow. The tail acts as a counterbalance to prevent over-rotation, and, by arching its back to

absorb some of the shock of hitting the ground, the cat can often land without injury.

However, cats are not infallible. City vets are used to treating cats with 'high-rise syndrome' – cats that have fallen off balconies or out of windows several storeys up. Some have remarkable escapes from death even then, but there are many serious injuries too. A very common injury is a broken jaw, which results from the sheer speed of the fall and the cat hitting its jaw on the ground as it lands on its feet. Nature only designed cats for short falls from trees, not long falls from tower blocks.

Owners who live in flats are still recommended to prevent cats from going on the balcony and to keep mesh over the windows. Apparently most falls happen when cats are distracted by birds or clouds passing by outside.

Why do cats get stuck up trees?

The cat's beautifully designed claws allow it to pull itself up trees very rapidly. It uses them like crampons and the curve of the claws means that there's little danger of them slipping out of the bark. However, when the cat tries to climb down this can cause a problem, because their claws just don't work in the same way on the way down. Very often the cat will have run up the tree in a panic to get away from something on the ground, and the adrenaline surge will have given them the strength to climb as high as possible.

Cats do learn to climb down, but they do it much less gracefully than when they're on the way up. When the cat reaches a certain distance from the ground it usually leaps off.

There's one tree-living species of wild cat that has unique double-jointed feet that can swivel around to point backward for the downward climb, which must be very useful!

prey so that the cat's line of sight isn't interrupted – the body carries the head along smoothly. Unlike our human shoulder blades, which lie flat on the back of the rib cage, the cat's shoulders swing along with its legs, giving it a greater range of movements and the ability to lengthen its legs.

The structure of a cat's body is therefore strong and flexible, with adaptations that allow it to move smoothly. But this isn't enough. It's the cat's control system that ensures swift response and action. Automatic responses and reactions and a fantastic sense of balance correct the cat's posture rapidly, so that it can right itself before losing its footing. It can even turn in mid-air during a fall, giving it a strong chance of landing on its feet and minimising the risk of injury, which means that it can leap and jump with confidence and safety.

Though the cat's body makes it strong it's built for sprinting rather than long-distance running. Thus a cat will stalk its prey until it's very close and then launch into a pounce. When they do run they're light on their feet. In fact cats walk and run on the feline equivalent of the tips of their toes, and by hitting the ground briefly and lengthening and shortening the spine they can attain considerable speed over short distances.

Cats also make use of the vertical spaces and perches around them, because they can leap to a considerable height – equivalent to us jumping up about 25ft (8m). They can also climb rapidly, using their fantastic claws like crampons. Coming down can be a little more difficult, though, because their claws are then pointing in the wrong direction. However, they usually manage!

The cat's armoury

So, the skeleton is specialised, the muscles are primed, the body is strong and supple, the reactions are like lightning, the eyes have super-sight and the ears can hear a pin

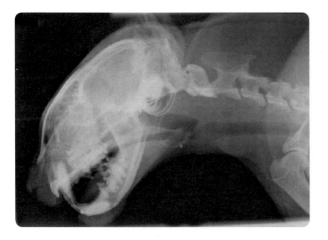

drop…the cat is ready. But in addition to all this the hunting machine now needs weapons with which to capture and kill efficiently.

When you look at the cat's skull the two most obvious features are its huge eye sockets and the short, strong jaws lined with sharp teeth. The large eye sockets are no surprise, knowing how important sight is to the cat in its hunting life. Although the cat has fewer teeth than other carnivores, they're sharp and strong. The tiny incisor teeth along the front are designed for ripping and scraping flesh from bones and also help to nibble parasites when grooming. The dagger-like canines are designed to hold and kill prey. The molars slice meat into pieces small enough to swallow, as cats can't chew in the same way that people do.

What a beautiful design the cat's feet are! For silent running they can sheath the long and razor-sharp claws that are attached to the end of each last toe bone. Then, when they're needed, the claws are rapidly unsheathed from under the fold of skin by rotating the bones forwards, pushing out the claws. And they return to their silken purses just as smoothly. They're kept sharp by shedding the outer layers of the claw regularly to reveal gleaming new blades. Their backward-hooked shape allows the cat to grab prey and prevent it escaping while the teeth are brought into action. To make its claws even more effective the cat has a great deal of movement and twist in its front legs – compare them to the much more stiff front legs of a dog. Indeed, the cat's paws are more like a monkey's than those of other carnivores, and cats can also use them for grooming and to lift food that they can't reach with their mouths.

Of course, these weapons aren't just used offensively; they're frequently required when the cat needs to defend itself.

How do cats sharpen their claws?

When we see cats clawing at tree trunks, furniture or carpets we say that they're 'sharpening their claws'. But how does this work?

A cat's claws shouldn't be thought of as hooks but as an elegant, sophisticated system that provides the cat with an ever-sharp set of rapiers. Its claws are actually protractile rather than retractable – that is, they're normally sheathed in little velvet pockets so that they don't catch on things as the cat walks through the undergrowth, and also so that their tips aren't blunted and are kept razor-sharp for hunting. In addition they're well provided with nerves,

Use proper clippers and trim claws with care if it needs to be done.

which give the cat information about the extension of the claws and their movement sideways. All of which means that a cat's claws aren't merely inert nails used as simple weapons; they're sensitive tools that give the cat a great deal of extremely useful information in addition to their obvious uses of catching and holding prey and climbing.

When we talk about claw sharpening we don't mean the equivalent of knife sharpening, where the edge is ground until it's sharp. Instead, the claw is actually renewed, and the process of 'sharpening' is actually the shedding of an old layer of claw to reveal a sharp new one underneath. If you look at where your cat strops or sharpens its claws you'll find little white, crescent-shaped pieces that are the outer layer of claw that's come off.

Incidentally, unlike our fingernails a cat's claws are actually attached to their bones, so that when people 'de-claw' cats they're actually removing the equivalent of the end of the finger. This practice isn't allowed in the UK but occurs in the USA and many other countries.

Some owners clip their cat's claws so that they're a little less sharp and do less damage if they scratch the furniture or carpets. However, this needs to be done with care, as there's a blood vessel (known as the quick) inside which will bleed if the claw is clipped too short. Purchase proper cat claw clippers for the task, then sit quietly with the cat, being firm but gentle. Cut below where you see the quick. If you're unsure you could ask your vet or veterinary nurse to give you a lesson initially.

As is so often the case, getting your cat used to having its claws clipped while it's still a kitten will make it much more amenable to the process than if you only start when it's an adult. Some cats will put up with it, others won't. If your cat lives a very active outdoor life this will blunt its claws anyway, and most owners will find that clipping isn't necessary. However, as a cat gets older it may not be so active and may not care for its claws so well. These may then grow overlong and curl around into the pads, so owners of older cats should check their feet regularly and clip their claws if necessary.

Putting it all together: cat the superhunter

A feral cat – one that lives a wild lifestyle without any human help – has to go from birth to becoming an efficient and self-sufficient hunter in a very short period of time – less than six months. It has to learn not only to control and make the best of the talents genetics have given it, but also to hone its hunting techniques while learning about the great wide world, and how to avoid danger while getting itself out there in order to make about ten kills a day.

Armed with those fantastic claws and its teeth the cat can either position itself along the route of a small mammal and wait for it to come along, or can creep up on it. Either way the cat needs to fix the small mammal or bird with its claws and then get it into position to kill it. Bear in mind that a cat sees best when the object it's focusing on is between 2m and 6m away (6–20ft), and that its vision is not as good when the prey is closer to its face.

It has to use its 'third hand' – its whiskers – to help it. These can be pitched right forward to touch the prey and help the cat to understand how it's orientated and how far away it is. When the sensitive skin and hairs around the mouth come into contact with the prey they set off a sequence of automatic movements. These turn the cat's head and position it to make the killing bite. Another set of receptors along the lips make the jaws open, more receptors in the mouth trigger the bite itself. In a successful nape bite the canine tooth slips between the neck bones and severs the prey's spinal cord. Death is instantaneous. The canine teeth and the claws are also sense organs in that they can tell the cat how much resistance or pressure they're meeting with. Hunting requires rapid reactions, so such automatic signals mean that no time is lost. Split seconds could mean the difference between feasting and starving.

So this is the fantastic creature that is the cat. If we understand all of this it will help us enormously in placing it within the context of our world, and in realising how we impact upon it, both intentionally and unintentionally.

Above: Young ferel cats need to be self-sufficient at a very young age.

Right: Cats are good climbers and high places provide safe havens when necessary.

Below: Hunting requires concentration and skill.

FEELING SAFE, STAYING SAFE

What is territory?

We glibly say 'cats are territorial' and we know it means something about cats chasing other cats away from their garden, or being very upset if strange cats come into the house. We think we understand that they don't like having other cats around, but how deep does that feeling go? How important is it to cats, and why?

Remember that we're totally insignificant when it comes to how cats have developed and what's important to them. We may have lived alongside the cat for thousands of years, but millions of years of evolution have made it what it is and given it the genes that drive its behaviour. So, taking us out of the equation, a cat will survive on it own wits and talents.

Cats have come from solitary ancestors, although they can and do live in groups if there's enough food around for them to do so (which usually means in places where man has left food or has resources which attract the cat's prey, such as grain stores). However, usually they have to carve out an area which has the potential to feed them and, if the cat is female, to provide her with enough prey to feed her kittens as well. This is a very precious resource, and the term 'territory' could be defined as the area a cat is prepared to defend for these reasons. The cat may range further afield than this, but probably can't defend a larger area. The greater the abundance of prey available, the smaller the area the cat needs to defend, as defence requires energy and sometimes physical risk in seeing off other cats.

The cat is on its own when it comes to hunting and survival – there's no pack of like-minded creatures to back it up and make it feel secure, as there would be for a dog. So the cat is careful and alert to intrusion.

Female cats (queens) will defend an area for themselves and their kittens that's usually smaller than the range of male cats (toms). An unneutered tom will keep other cats away from an area containing queens he might mate with. As a source of food and mates, territory is pretty vital to cats and is taken exceptionally seriously.

Bear this 'natural' feline existence in mind when you transport the cat into our human world and into our homes and gardens. Inside that brain still shrieks the same territorial defender. Here a cat's territory is usually the safe core inside the house and then the garden. Because there's an abundance of food and because most of our pet cats are neutered, this may be enough for many cats. However, in an area where there are large numbers of cats these territories may overlap considerably and competition may be fierce. The weather or season may also affect how far and how often cats go outside the home and into the garden territory. When the weather is warm and there are lots of little prey animals around to stimulate the cat's natural hunting instincts, it may move further afield more frequently.

When we introduce new cats into a home where there's already a cat we need to remember what an intrusion this is, and how instinctive the reaction of the resident cat may be – it's not jealousy or being difficult that stops it welcoming a new cat with open arms, it's instinct and survival. But more of this later.

How do cats tell other cats they're there?

As a social animal we humans tend to think that our cats might be lonely on their own, or that they'll want another cat to keep them company. However, when you look at how they communicate with other cats you'll see that most of the signals they use are telling the other cats to keep away, rather than welcoming them in to share a mouse.

A cat can't be present at all times at all points in its territory (indeed, it can't even see all of it), so it has to have a mechanism for taking possession and telling other cats that this area is in use. This can be done using scent marking, so that the cat doesn't need to meet or confront other cats. Coming face to face can lead to aggression or fighting, which in turn can cause injury or lead to life-threatening infection, so it's much better to bluff it out with scent. As well as leaving messages for other cats, the scents cats leave also make them feel 'at home' in their own territory.

Of course, there are occasions when cats do actually want to get together – for the making of more cats in particular! When a female cat is in season and ready for mating she needs to find a mate. Therefore she needs to let the toms in the area know they're welcome and won't be chased off if they appear. She can do this in several different ways, by making a noise – or 'calling' as it's known – and by leaving scent messages that can be sensed a long way off.

This is the reason cats have an excellent sense of smell; there are complex messages to be left and understood. Cats can leave them in several different ways, some more subtle than others. The messages relayed by means of scent contain information about sex, reproductive status, health, strength, when the message was last made and all sorts of other things.

To us the cat is much less smelly animal than the dog – one of the pleasures of cats is that, to us, they don't smell. But this merely emphasises how different we are and how insensitive we are to scent. However, the cat has quite a few sources of smell available to it and each of these is used a little differently.

Certain areas of skin on the cat's chin, lips, temples, neck, shoulders and at the base of its tail have special sebaceous glands that produce an oily secretion which has

a scent specific to that cat – its own signature smell. As the cat grooms, it not only keeps its coat in tip-top condition but also spreads the secretions from these glands all over its coat. When the cat rubs itself against objects around the home, other cats, the dog, a fence and even us, it smears them with some of this scent. Also by rubbing its chin and mouth along objects (one of those classic cat movements it

Left: Using glands around the mouth, the cat rubs scent onto familiar objects.

Above: Cats are sensitive to smells we cannot even imagine!

Below: Feeling threatened and uncomfortable this cat tries not to be noticed.

often does to us) it anoints them with secretions directly from the glands around the mouth. This has a special name – bunting. The cat seems to enjoy this action, perhaps because the scents it leaves behind give it a feeling of wellbeing and of being 'at home', surrounded by the comfort of its own scent. It could be likened to us putting the ornaments, pictures and special bits and pieces around our homes that make them personal to us.

Another source of scent is the glands around the pads on the cat's paws – they secrete a type of sweat that keeps the pads oiled so that they remain sensitive and supple. So when a cat scratches it claws along a tree trunk (or the sofa!) it leaves a scent mark as well as the physical scratch mark.

Cats can also use urine and faeces to leave messages. Normally they would dig a hole to deposit waste so that it's hidden and doesn't give their position away, but cats can also use their waste to highlight their presence or to mark their territory. Leaving faeces out in the open is called middening, and is a ploy that's used by many animals.

The cat has a very efficient way of using urine to send out strong and long-lasting messages. These messages are positioned at nose level so that they're obviously to any cat that walks past and can also be dispersed further by the wind. Urine passed on the ground may seep away and be covered over by other smells from the earth. It's also too low to be picked up and carried by air currents. So the cat overcomes this by spraying its urine. Both male and female cats can and do spray. To do this they take up a very characteristic position with tail held high. A quivering action follows, accompanied by a paddling or treading motion with the back feet. Urine is squirted backwards and

hits whatever is behind the cat several inches off the ground – most importantly at nose height for other passing cats. As these scent markings fade they're regularly topped up, to keep them potent and the message clear.

Top of the charts for 'make you notice' smells, and one which even we scent-retarded humans can appreciate, is unneutered tom spray. This 'eau de tom' contains secretions from the anal glands and is very strong. It does decompose slowly and loses its impact over time, but it's unforgettable.

If cats do get within sight of each other they have a range of body language that will back up the scent messages. Unlike dogs, which live in a social group and must fit into and take account of how they interact with other dogs that have a different status within the group, cats don't have a hierarchy but must interact according to

personality – strong or nervous, despotic or friendly. Thus cats don't have a similar range of body postures and facial expressions that can convey submission or dominance, compliance or friendliness, as happens in a dog pack. The repertoire of the cat is much more limited, although we probably miss most of the subtle signals which do pass between them. So at a very basic level cats may hunch down and draw in whiskers, ears, limbs and tail to make themselves small and less likely to be noticed, and to seem less threatening. If pushed they may try to bluff it out by looking as large as possible – standing sideways on with hair erect and fluffed up to try and prevent attack. The pictures on pages 26 and 27 show facial and body postures that are typical of cats conveying different messages.

Cementing a group: living together

As was explained earlier, cats have solitary ancestors but they can live in groups, as we see with feral cats if there are enough resources (food and den areas). Our pet cats too often live with another cat or cats, sometimes successfully, sometimes not. We've also explored the scent messages cats leave to keep other cats at bay. But what about when they do enjoy the company of other cats – how do they behave in this situation?

Scent can also be used to bond; the familiarity can help cats to feel secure and relaxed. To cats, our homes smell,

Above: Cats that live together will have a group scent.

the dog smells, we smell, and as we live together and pat and cuddle each other we mix all of these smells to produce a group scent which the cat will recognise.

Inside our homes cats will rub their chins and faces around the furniture and each other, and of course cats

29

that get on will often groom each other. That's the ultimate in scent mixing and sampling – tasting, even.

We've come to understand these scents a little better recently because scientists have studied them and even managed to make synthetic scents based on what they found. These are now being used in homes, veterinary surgeries and other places where cats might feel under stress, to help them to relax. How does this work? It's thought that the scents that cats leave when they rub their faces on our furniture give them a feeling of wellbeing and are a signal that they can relax because this is a safe area.

If a strange cat comes into your home and sprays you'll notice how upsetting it is for your own cats. Their safe indoor den has been violated by an outsider. This can prompt a resident cat into spraying indoors itself to restore the status quo and its own sense of 'familiar'.

When you try to introduce a new cat into your home to be a 'friend' to your resident cat you need to try and understand the invasion it represents, and scent can be used as a tool to try and move the relationship forward. Among other things, the new cat will need to take on the 'group smell' before it's accepted, and this may take some time.

Understanding this smell of home also helps us to understand the insecurity that can come to a cat if we change the furniture or the carpet or redecorate – removing familiar scents as well as introducing strong new ones. Using strong disinfectants or pine scents can also overcome the more subtle scents that a cat has laid down.

How do cats live close to other cats if they want to?

Cats that get on have a different set of body language to those that don't. What will be most evident is how relaxed friendly cats are with each other, and how tense cats become when they don't get on.

With cats, behaviour is not often overt. Hissing and fighting are at the extreme end of the scale and are pretty easy to understand. However, a lot of the time cats that don't get on simply sit quietly and are very subdued, so that they don't attract attention or invite attack. They move around carefully and quietly and check rooms carefully before they enter, in case the other cat is there. More subtle body postures and eye and ear signals can be seen, but to us busy people the fact that the cats are living in the same house without fighting means that they're the best of friends. Often this isn't the case. There may be stand-offs at the food bowl or at the litter tray or when cats come in and out of the cat flap. In the next chapter we'll see how you can plan where the cats' resources are put so that they're not placed in a competitive situation when they go to use them.

The best example of friendly cat behaviour can be seen in the most obvious place – between mothers and kittens.

And kittens, being young and enthusiastic, have exaggerated body language not refined by adult sensibility. So watching kittens can be like reading a book with big writing and pictures – it's all laid out in its simplest form for us to see.

Watch how kittens greet their mother as she comes back to see them. Tail up, they'll greet her nose-to-nose, rub alongside her, sniff her and they may even purr. Head and body rubbing will reinforce scent bonds. Lying together and grooming are all good signs. Cats that get on will seek each other out to cuddle up together, to play, and are happy to eat alongside each other.

Usually groups of feral cats comprise related females and their kittens. Young males will stay for a while and then move on to find their own territories.

Even neighbouring cats which are competitive over territory can operate a type of 'time share' in the garden, as they don't want to have to face

Sniffing is an important part of recognition.

An ill cat may need time to recouperate before greeting the resident cat.

each other every day and undergo a lengthy battle of wills. Because of the risk of injury cats will try not to let most 'battles' end in physical fighting but will vie by means of staring matches, or leave scent messages which other cats can interpret in terms of avoiding one another.

Some cats may be good 'friends'. You can see by the way they approach each other – standing tall, head up, tail high, going nose to tail and nose to nose with the other cat – that they don't fear each other. Once they've checked each other out just to make sure, they're very comfortable and may groom, play or cuddle up together.

However, as explained in Chapter 4, cats don't just rely on sight for recognition, and scent is vitally important. A breakdown in relationships between cats that have lived together happily for years can occur when one is removed from the household for a time and comes back smelling very different. This often happens when a cat is ill and has to spend time in a veterinary hospital. It comes back smelling very alien, and may also be behaving out of character if it's had an operation or is on some type of medication. Owners report that the cat that stayed at home sniffs the homecoming cat and reacts aggressively. Their relationship can break down very seriously. The returning cat's scent profile is more important than its physical presence, which is not recognised without the back-up confirmation of the right scent. It's sometimes hard for us humans, who have a terrible sense of smell compared to dogs and cats, to understand the strength of this instinct and the immediate and strong reactions that it can trigger.

There are things you can do to help:

■ Bring the returning cat back in a basket lined with a blanket that smells of home, so that it begins to take on a familiar scent again.

■ Don't put the cats together immediately. Let the returning cat settle in and start to take on the scent of home but keep it in a separate room. You can speed up the scent mixing process by grooming or stroking one cat and then the other. Concentrate around the face area (where there are lots of scent glands) and mix the scents up. As the returning cat loses the smell of the veterinary surgery it will also start to take on scents that the home cat is comfortable and familiar with.

■ Don't rush. Take your time and let the cats adapt slowly. If the returning cat has been feeling ill or had an operation it may feel vulnerable or reactive and will need to settle in without having to feel defensive.

Cats who get on are happy to cuddle up together.

WHY DO CATS . . .?

Understanding those feline foibles

Cats are mysterious creatures – this is one of the reasons why they hold such a great fascination for us. They see life from a totally different point of view to us. However, in our efforts to understand them we often anthropomorphise their behaviour, finding human reasons for some of the things they do. This chapter collects together some of the many questions often asked about cats and why they do what they do, and how what we do to control (or try to control) their lives impacts on them. It's a rather random collection of questions, but taken together they help us towards a better understanding of what it's like to be or to live with a cat.

Why do cats purr?

Purring is an extraordinary habit and we aren't entirely sure exactly how cats do it. And not just domestic cats purr – many of the larger members of the cat family can also generate this rhythmic vibration. To owners it's a most rewarding sound, perhaps because we understand that cats only do it at particular times and it's somehow special. The experience is both auditory and physical.

But perhaps the reason we like it is even more instinctive that that. Cats purr at a constant frequency of 25 cycles per second, and laid on top of this rhythm is the additional timing of the cat's breathing. It feels almost like a heartbeat and is certainly very relaxing and pleasurable. Additionally, we're pleased because the cat is relaxed enough to exhibit this behaviour to us.

Indeed, purring stems from kittenhood. While the cat is a predator, it's also a very small one and is vulnerable to becoming prey itself. Therefore having small kittens can be a very dangerous time – the mother is more vulnerable because she has to be in the den nursing the kittens, and she also has to hunt more, so that she can feed herself in order to produce milk, and later to provide food for the kittens. The kittens too are vulnerable, because they're even smaller and she has to leave them for periods to hunt. When she comes back to the den she'll signal to the kittens that everything's OK by purring. They in turn can suck and purr at the same time, letting her know that they're well. How reassuring it must be for the kittens, sucking milk within the warm coat of their mother in a den echoing with the sound of purring – utter contentment!

Cats also purr when they're injured or ill. Perhaps this is an attempt to reproduce that feeling of reassurance and safety that usually accompanies purring. Some people even suggest that purring itself has healing qualities and keeps the body healthy. This may be true, but we don't have any scientific evidence for it.

Left: Recent research shows that cats have a solicitation purr which varies from the contentment purr in that it has a high frequency element which triggers a sense of urgency in the human brain.

Why do cats knead with their claws?

When kittens are suckling from their mother they knead with their paws to stimulate the milk flow from the mammary gland down into the teats. Sitting on our laps when they're older, full-grown cats will often purr (another kitten behaviour) at the same time as they pad us. Some will even dribble at this point, proving the link between these behaviours: the kneading is still associated with feeding in the cat's mind, and it consequently causes the cat to salivate in anticipation of a milky meal.

Whether cats view us humans as 'mothers' in this situation isn't really understood. However, we should be flattered when they feel relaxed enough in our company to revert to this kittenish behaviour.

Kneading is a kittens behaviour to stimulate milk flow.

Why do cats have rougher tongues than dogs?

A cat has much more control over itself than a dog in all sorts of ways. This includes brushing or combing itself all over and keeping itself clean. It has a remarkable tool for this – its tongue, which has several important jobs. As an inbuilt comb, the tongue is covered with hook-shaped barbs that face backwards. When pulled through the fur these part it and remove dead hair, debris and parasites to keep the coat in perfect condition and lying flat, in order that the cat can tell when it's ruffled or disturbed. These barbs also allow the cat to literally lick meat off bone if it needs to.

Of course, the tongue is also the cat's organ of taste, as well as being spoon-shaped to lap up water – a genuine multi-purpose organ. When a cat licks you the roughness of its tongue is very evident.

Why do cats play with their prey?

Cat owners are never very happy to see their cats playing with prey, especially if it's still alive – it seems so cruel. It's been suggested that cats play more with 'dangerous' prey such as rats in order to practise manipulation and handling while avoiding getting bitten. Or it may be that the cat hasn't managed to inflict the killing bite, or hasn't learned how to do it properly and so can't quite reach that final stage quickly and cleanly. Movement is then necessary in order to maintain the cat's interest in killing the prey, and throwing it around causes movement. Of course, it could be that cats simply enjoy the hunting game.

Why do some cats miaow when others don't?

Researchers have noted some 16 different vocal patterns in cats, although individual cats may add their own personal sounds that they only use with their owners. Cats don't make sounds in the same way as we do. They can vocalise and breathe in and out at the same time, so don't use their tongue to form sounds in the same way as humans. The sounds are instead made farther back in the throat by the cat pushing air over its vocal cords at different speeds, and by changing the tension in its throat it alters the phonetic quality of the noises.

Most of the sounds cats make fall into three groups: the purr or little chirp they make when they greet us; the sounds they make when they're fearful or emotionally charged, such as hissing, spitting, sounds of pain, the yowelling of toms and the calling of females in season; and miaows. Cats can manipulate the miaow sound to make it very different in different circumstances – they can make it pleading or angry, welcoming or accusatory.

Individual cats vary in how much they 'talk' with us. Some breeds are notably noisier than others – the Siamese tops the list of chatty cats, with other breeds such as the Burmese also being pretty talkative.

There are huge variations between the 'conversation' levels of individual cats, and part of this is linked to how much *we* talk to *them*. If, when they miaow to us, we reply or ask them what they want, and their communication is answered with something rewarding, such as attention or food, then they're very likely to do the same thing again. Indeed, in this way *they* train *us* to respond, and reward us with a conversation.

Most of us love our cats to talk to us and encourage interaction. The most appealing communication of all is the 'silent miaow', where the cat goes through the mouth-opening motions of miaowing but no sound comes out – perhaps the most compelling plea of all. Just why or how they do the silent miaow isn't really understood, but if we respond to it that's enough to encourage them to do it again!

Why do cats have a mad half-hour?

Good question! We've already seen that the usual hunting strategy of cats is to get as close as possible by stealth and then launch into an explosive leap or sprint to surprise and catch their prey. When you see a cat jump many times its own height you realise what a strong and lithe body it needs to have. Indeed, the cat has many amazing senses and talents hidden under that furry exterior. It can be lightning fast when necessary, and is capable of astonishing flexibility that enables it to groom every part of its body except its face and the back of its head.

All of this is programmed into your pet cat. When it's young and learning it's like any other young creature, full of energy and easily excited. But cats are like Ferraris – finely tuned, powerful and easy to put into a spin. Perhaps all of its enthusiasm and boundless energy just overflows now and again and the cat has a mad half-hour when it can't contain itself. It's also good exercise and a chance to try out muscles and acceleration that wouldn't be used if it was just lying around in the house.

And it's not just young cats that climb the wall and curtains. Older cats can have a mad half-hour too. Somehow it's much more amusing when the oldies do it and behave like the mad kittens they once were. Perhaps they don't go up the curtains any more – mostly because the curtains would probably fall down with their weight on them – but they can still run rings around the furniture!

Why do cats hate travelling in the car?

As we've seen, cats love their territory, usually more than their owners. Therefore unlike a dog, which is used to going off-territory and is desperate to stay with its pack (or pack replacement – its owners) wherever it goes, cats don't like going off-territory, as it makes them feel vulnerable. They're not really reassured much by our presence either, which doesn't help them predict what will happen in this new territory or reassure them that we'll protect them. Cats may also be more sensitive to the movement of the car – their sense of balance is very acute, so the motion may not be pleasant to them, and they may not feel in control of the situation. The car will also sound and smell very strange.

All of these things make the cat feel very stressed. Bear in mind also that your cat probably only goes in the car when you take it either to the vet or the cattery, and so associates it with going somewhere that's strange and beyond its comfort zone. However, many breeders take their cats around the country to shows, and some cats do seem to get used to travelling. The occasional cat also seems to enjoy travelling on holiday with its owner, so it's not all negative. Like lots of other things, if travelling in cars starts in kittenhood – when a cat doesn't have so much fear and takes everything in its stride – it can even become accepted as being normal.

Why is it difficult to train a cat?

Dogs do as they're told – if they're trained; but cats seldom do as they're told and we don't train them. Does this mean dogs are more intelligent that cats? Yet a cat could step from being a pet to surviving in the wild without missing a beat; perhaps *that's* a true sign of intelligence. Perhaps intelligence is *not* doing things that seem to have no purpose just because someone's telling you to.

If we're to judge animals by how they react to us trying to train them, then we have to think about how we actually do that, and what motivates an animal to actually do our bidding. In order to get another creature to do something, we need it first to understand our desire and then to actually want to do it. For dogs there are lots of motivations. As social creatures, they gain reward and probably a 'feel good factor' from being around us, their replacement pack. Attention is reward to them, as is feeling themselves to be part of the gang; and, of course, so is food – a great motivator for most canines. But what motivates a cat? Perhaps a favourite treat – a prawn or smoked salmon? Sometimes, sometimes not. What about attention? Sometimes, depending on the cat, and sometimes not!

But people do train cats – they can jump through fiery hoops, they can sit on command and they'll come when they're called.

Why do cats chatter their teeth?

Teeth-chattering is a very curious sound which cats make, though you may never actually hear your cat do it. The best chance to hear it is when there's a bird outside the window, perhaps on a birdfeeder, which the cat is watching but can't get to. It may then run up to the window or sit and make this strange tooth-chattering noise, which may be excitement or frustration or both – we don't really know why.

Why don't cats like having their tummy tickled?

A cat is pretty well armed at all four corners and at the front as well. Combine this armoury with speed of movement and you have an animal that can defend itself very well, as long as it's facing its threat and can use its weapons. However, the stomach area is a very vulnerable spot – damage this and you can get to the vital organs and cause life-threatening injury. Consequently cats are naturally very protective of their stomach and some don't like anyone to touch this area. It's the sign of a relaxed and trusting cat if it lets you tickle its tummy.

Some cats tolerate or even enjoy their tummies tickled – to others it is a no go area.

Why do cats grab your hand when you stroke their tummy?

The answer to this question follows on from the previous one. Even a cat that's relaxed and generally lets you stroke or tickle its tummy may suddenly feel vulnerable, and when it does its automatic defence mechanism is activated. It then goes into 'grab the hand and kick with the back legs' mode without even really thinking about it.

If you have a cat which does this the secret is to only stroke its tummy for a very brief period and to stop before the cat reacts – in that way it doesn't reach that reactive state and each little interaction is relaxing and pleasurable. Watch its face carefully – if its ears start to fold backwards, its tail slowly twitches or its pupils dilate so that the eyes seem to go black, it may be starting to react. These are all telltale signs that doubt is creeping into the cat's mind about being so vulnerable. So you have to learn to 'read' your cat and its behaviour – which can be fun and very satisfying.

Why do cats eat grass?

Even though cats are obligate carnivores and don't usually volunteer to eat fruit and vegetables, they do like to chew grass, and it's part of their normal behavioural repertoire. Whether it helps to move food or hairballs through the digestive tract (up or down!), or gives them some vitamins/trace elements that they need, we're not really sure.

However, cats do like to have the opportunity to chew grass and it's particularly important to make it available to indoor cats. You can bring some in from the garden, buy grass seeds to grow or buy a cat grass pack from the pet store. Cats that don't have access to grass or other harmless herbs may be driven to sample plants which they normally wouldn't touch, and this can lead to the ingestion of harmful pot plants or cut flowers, such as lilies (see page 114). For this reason it's always sensible to remove any plants which could be dangerous to indoor cats and give them access to safe ones such as grass, catnip or other suitable herbs. The Feline Advisory Bureau has a list of poisonous plants on its website at www.fabcats.org.

Although cats are carnivores, they do need access to grass to chew.

Why do cats hate sprays?

Luckily, these days we have excellent flea treatments for cats that are applied to the skin at the back of the neck (see pages 98 and 104). However, in the not too distant past we treated cat fleas by means of sprays, often containing organophosphates, and the mere sight of the spray-can sent most cats streaking off under the bed or out into the garden.

Cats really seem to hate sprays. There may be a couple of reasons for this. Firstly, when cats are feeling threatened and pushed into a corner, or if they're startled, they hiss. It's an explosive noise. The action reveals a gaping pink mouth and teeth which are hard to ignore, and the animal or person that's provoked it can feel the air passing as the cat hisses. So cats don't really appreciate the equivalent of a hiss close to them. Secondly, they have a very sensitive force field of hairs over the body that helps the cat 'feel' where it is – very useful if you hunt in the dark. A spray will set these touch receptors off, and the cat may not understand or enjoy the sensation. The chemicals in the spray are also likely to smell very strong to the scent-sensitive cat.

A hiss in a can! Cats avoid sprays if at all possible.

How do you keep a cat off the garden?

Cats always know who has the best-kept garden with the softest soil and nothing will beat a well-tended vegetable patch as a perfect latrine. This can be very irritating and somewhat off-putting when you want fresh vegetables, but the cats aren't doing it to annoy you. They're doing it because you've made that particular patch of soil very attractive to them. Cats naturally dig a hole in soil in which to deposit their urine or faeces and then cover it up. So if its own patch of ground is frozen, rock hard, impacted or paved then the cat has to go elsewhere to find a substrate which will allow it to fulfil its natural needs.

People try lots of things to keep cats off gardens. Among these are putting pruned branches from spiky plants around and over the patch, especially as seedlings come through; leaving empty plastic fizzy-drink bottles around (I don't know why this is supposed to work, but some people say it does); planting *Coleous canina* around the patch (this is the so called 'Scaredy-cat' plant, which is said to be offensive to cats and is available from garden centres); sprinkling commercially available cat deterrents (though these can get washed away when it rains); and having a cat or dog of their own which keeps other cats out of the garden (rather excessive perhaps, but it works well).

If you're planning well ahead you could actually put chicken wire over the soil once you've planted the seeds; this prevents the cat from digging up the soil and the seedlings can grow through it very successfully. Other people use ultrasonic cat deterrents – again, these may or may not work but might be worth a try. The theory is that

The best tended gardens provide cats with the perfect litter tray!

they produce a high-pitched sound (at a frequency above that which we can hear) that's supposed to be unpleasant for the cat, so that it goes elsewhere. Providing cats with an area of well-tilled soil or sand away from the main vegetable plot may also help.

Remember to cover children's sandpits or sandboxes when they're not being used. For a cat these are the most tempting toilet of all, as they have nice soft sand which is easy to dig in, so you can't blame a cat for taking this option if it's available to them.

How do you make a cat's first excursion outside as safe as possible?

If you've got a new adult cat, the first step is to keep it indoors for several weeks to bond it to the house before you let it go out for the first time. If you've got a kitten, you can think about letting it out once it's had all of its vaccinations and has been neutered and has recovered. At this point it will probably be about five months old and still quite small, so initially it's best to try and control when it goes out. Depending on where you live and what the risks in the garden might be, you might only want to let it out when you can go out with it, so that it doesn't get itself into trouble. Make sure that both cat and kitten know how to use the cat flap if that's the route by which they'll go out and come in (see page 82), or they might feel that they're stuck outside. If the weather is nice you could just open the door and potter in the garden with the kitten.

It's useful to get the cat or kitten used to being called to come to you – you can do this by offering it little treats so that it's happy to respond. You then have a little bit of control when you go outside to call them in.

Choose a quiet time of day to let them out for the first time. Excitements such as other cats, dogs which might bark, or children screaming in the neighbour's garden, are best avoided for the first couple of excursions, so that your cat can concentrate on you and isn't spooked. Go outside for just a very quick walk around the garden and then call the cat or kitten in again, giving it a treat. You may want to do this just before feeding time, or even hold off feeding it so that the cat is a little hungry and therefore keen to follow you back inside in the expectation of a meal. You want it to be calm and happy to be out with you and to learn to find its way back.

Gradually let it out for a little longer and to venture a little further. Of course, there are always some risks outside which you can try and minimise – perhaps by putting up a fence to keep the cat off the road (older cats probably won't try to scale great heights to go further afield the way that young cats may do). Try to get the cat into the routine of coming in at night too.

Some people take on adult cats that have never been outside before and wonder if they'll be able to adapt to going out into the big wide world. But it's amazing how adaptable cats are, and there are many examples of cats that have led an indoor existence for most of their lives relishing the opportunity to go outside in a new environment. They may be a little nervous at first, but most take to it like a duck to water. Some even do some hunting, and it's fascinating to think that all of this instinctive behaviour has lain dormant yet can still spring to life when the cat gets the opportunity to do what it was built to do.

What's the best way to move house with cats?

Moving house is supposedly one of the most stressful times in one's life, and it's not just keeping the house tidy while waiting for a buyer, or successfully reaching completion and doing all the packing, that bring on the trauma. Ensuring that the cat's safely caught before he cottons on that something's happening and vanishes, and then introducing him to the new neighbourhood when you get there, are certain to make the tension last a bit longer!

Cats often have a sixth sense that something's going to happen when you're moving house. In reality they're picking up all sorts of cues from you, such as changes in routine, mood, excitement and anxiety, strange-smelling boxes and furniture where it doesn't normally sit. If this unsettles them they may go and find somewhere where they can feel secure until it's safe to come out – which, of course, may be after the furniture van and family have driven away! So if you're moving, among all of those other things you need to organise, think about the cat.

If you're not moving far you may want to put the cat into a cattery a few days before, and bring it to your new home a few days after the move, when the furniture's in place and some semblance of normality is returning. However, if you're moving a long distance this is less practical, as you'd have to come back to pick up the cat, so it's normally easiest to take it with you.

Think ahead, and keep the cat in the night before the move so that it doesn't vanish at the last minute. Find a quiet room on move day where you can shut the door, and the cat can stay in there quiet and secure – a bathroom is often useful, as there's little to move out (as long as you have another toilet for

everyone to use). Make sure there's a sign on the door warning everyone that the cat's inside. Put its usual bed in there, with a litter tray and a little food (you don't want the cat to have a big meal before taking it on a journey); and then the household can get on with everything else.

When everything's on the van, put the cat in its basket (it's best to have that ready in the 'quiet room' too, with a familiar-smelling piece of clothing or bedding in it), and then put it in the car for the journey.

If you're going on a long journey you may have to stop and offer it the use of a litter tray and some water. Make sure that you do this within the safe confines of the car, and ensure that all the windows are shut before you let the cat out of its carrier – it would be even worse to lose the cat along the way than leaving it at the old house! If you're travelling on a hot day make sure the cat doesn't overheat in the carrier if it's stuffed down between various other items in the back of the car with the sun shining through. If you stop for a coffee don't leave the cat in a shut car for even a few minutes if the sun's shining – the temperature

Below: Make sure the cat is safely installed in its carrier and take it in the car (not in the removal van) to the new house.

inside can rocket very quickly and the cat could suffer from heatstroke. This is all common sense, but in the midst of everything else you have to think about during a move such things can get overlooked.

Once you arrive, it's usually suggested that cats should be kept indoors for about two weeks so that they bond to their new territory and feel secure in their new home before going outside. This will vary between cats – some confident cats may be happy to go out in a few days, not being panicked by the new surroundings and happy to find their way back into the house. Others may need longer before they and their owners feel confident about letting them out.

Some cats are much better about staying indoors than others. If you have one of these indoor cats you may have to be more active and interactive with it, and play hunting and food-finding games to help release some of its pent-up energy and satisfy its hunting drive. You can try taking it outside using a harness, but many adult cats don't react terribly well to being restrained in this way – it's something usually best to start young. If you do want to try, then get the cat used to it indoors first and only try it outside when it's quiet so that there's nothing to panic them; not being able to run away can be very stressful, and having a whirling dervish on the end of a lead can be pretty scary! See also page 136.

If your new house is near the old one and the cat is likely to overlap its old territory or routes, it may well go back to your old home, and this may happen no matter how long you keep the cat inside. So make your new home as attractive as possible – give the cat a warm, cosy bed and

Keep your cat inside for two weeks if you can, so that it bonds to the new house.

lots of small meals to keep it interested in being around you. Use Feliway (a synthetic cat pheromone available from vets, which seems to make cats feel more confident and relaxed) to help bond them to the new house.

How do you stop a cat hunting?

If you've read the rest of this manual you'll have realised that a cat looks like it does and behaves like it does because it's a hunter. Millions of years of evolution have given it the senses and the body to be very successful at this. Obviously, therefore, we can't remove this drive, but we can try to control it a little by altering the times we let our cats out – for example by keeping them in at dawn and dusk when small creatures are most active.

Birds, of course, are active during the day and we attract them to our gardens with food during the winter months, giving the cat a very tempting focus of activity. So it's up to us to try and protect the birds that we're feeding and attracting. Some of this is practical – make sure the bird table is high enough to prevent easy access for the cat, have it on a pole which is difficult to climb and place it away from structures the cat could use to get on to it. Position it away from bushes or other places where the cat can hide. If you're hanging up a feeder put it on a bracket or branch which the cat can't access.

You may be aware of a study by the RSPB looking at

whether bells or ultrasonic devices on collars can help to cut down the number of prey animals caught by cats. Sometimes this seems like a very 'them' and 'us' topic. However, if you think that supporters of cats and birds are two distinct groups who never speak to each other you'd actually be very wrong. Indeed, the RSPB asked the advice of organisations such as the Feline Advisory Bureau and the RSPCA when they were putting the study together, to ensure that the collars they used were safe and that the cats were chosen carefully. They also recruited some of the cats that tried the collars through their own members – many, many cat owners are bird lovers too. Animal welfare organisations were very interested in the results of the survey and probably delighted that it was the RSPB who funded and ran it. Carrying out such a study properly and scientifically is no small task and requires considerable financial investment.

If you look at the way many cats hunt, they stay still or move very slowly indeed until the final pounce, when, usually, it's too late to escape, so it seems dubious whether

a bell would work. However, the study showed that bells and an ultrasonic peeping device did indeed help cut down catches by a third to a half.

So, armed with this information, what should cat owners do? It does, of course, raise the thorny issue of collars and safety for the cats that wear them (see page 135 for a fuller discussion on collars), but the most important thing is to choose a safe one. You should also check out the bell. Some have tapering slits which can trap a cat's claw if, for example, it scratched its neck. Its a small detail, but the cat needs to be kept safe too.

Would a bell tinkling in the cat's ears all day long be cruel? In an ideal world cats wouldn't wear collars. However, many owners already need their cats to wear one as a means of carrying identification (if they stray or get run over someone may take the initiative and contact them), or to hold magnets or electronic devices to open the cat flap, so adding a bell won't add to the risk.

However, we don't live in isolation. Birds are already under pressure from many sides, from loss of habitat and from cars among many other things. The RSPB isn't blaming cats for the decline in bird numbers, but does acknowledge that they're one of the many factors that can put pressure on some species that are already under threat. If a bell does work – and the RSPB work suggests that it at least helps – then we need to look at our individual cats and balance the risks and the benefits. Many cats don't bother to catch anything. Others are keen hunters. Age too is a factor – keen one- to three-year-olds which have energy to burn and love the outdoors may well be candidates for a bell, while older cats that prefer hunting down their food bowl and the warmest spot for a snooze may not.

What about the ultimate solution to bird or animal safety –

keeping cats indoors? Again it's a choice of where you sit on the risks versus benefits issue. Personally I'd still rather let my cat outside, with risk to potential prey, risk to the cat and perhaps some additional risk associated with collar wearing and the annoyance of a tinkly bell. I still feel the benefits of the outdoor life and letting a cat be a cat stack up positively on the side of psychological wellbeing, exercise and independence. Everyone must make up their own mind based on knowing their cat and its habits, the risks to and from the environment where they live and what wildlife is around.

Above and below: Hunting is what cats do! However, owners try different things to prevent them being successful.

How can I introduce a new cat successfully?

Introducing a new cat or kitten to a household can be quite stressful, to all concerned. Indeed, it's usually easier to introduce a dog to a cat than a cat to a cat. This is because a cat won't view a dog as competition for resources – it might have to get used to its excited behaviour and learn to stand up to it to avoid being chased, but this usually happens very quickly and much more easily than we imagine. The cat–cat thing is much more difficult.

Understanding that many, many cats won't welcome a new cat with open arms is key to trying to integrate them and to getting them to end up as friends rather than enemies. Even very sociable cats will initially be extremely defensive about having a new cat in the house. Remember our 'natural' cat, which has to defend a territory so that it has enough resources to survive? Well, it's lurking just beneath the skin of our pampered pets. True, you provide more food than it could ever need and it has plenty of beds and dens, but instinctively the cat's alarm bells will still be ringing. Even where feral cats live in groups these usually consist of related females and their offspring (the males going off to do their own thing when they're old enough), and 'strange' cats would still be chased off.

So the first thing to ensure is that the resources you give your household of cats are adequate. If you read the sections in this book covering feeding and the siting of food and other resources (see page 79) you'll see that just putting out lots of plates of food together isn't necessarily the answer. Where you put the food, whether the cat feels that it's uncomfortable competing for it there or whether there's somewhere it can access it where it feels secure, how many litter trays you have and where you place them, can all help to reduce the feeling of being taken over. For the new cat, this will help overcome the difficulty of getting to the things it needs while encroaching into the very vital areas of the resident cat's territory. It's not easy for either cat, so you need to be sensitive and, most of all, patient. Both cats will also need places to which they can retire to relax.

Don't be tempted just to open the cat basket and let the new cat straight into the resident cat's home without any restrictions or to let them 'fight it out'. If you start badly you may never regain that opportunity to actually get them together. Cats aren't very forgiving, and once they think something is a threat they may react too fast to ever get over this point of view.

Think cat and think scent first. Your home will have a

Introductions can be make or break in feline relationships. Taking time to get it right can make all the difference.

scent 'profile' which is familiar and reassuring to your resident cat. It will consist of all those things that go on there, the dog, the kids, the hobby equipment, the cleaning materials, the food you like and so on, all mixed in with the scents your own cat has anointed the house with. All the corners of furniture will have been wiped by your cat's chin and face, the doorposts have been brushed by its coat, and the carpet will often bear the marks of claw

During the first week or so just keep the cats apart. Stroke one cat and then the other; take a soft cotton cloth and wipe it around the new cat's face and under its chin and dab this around the house at cat-head level. You want to integrate the house scents with the new cat's smell so that it doesn't stand out as completely alien but has scent notes that are familiar to the resident cat. This takes a bit of time, but it will give the new cat an opportunity to get used to you and its surroundings so that it isn't quite so stressed. You can have one cat in a room and then swap it with the other, but don't let them meet initially. Some behaviourists say it's useful to let them see each other through a glass door so that their presence becomes a bit more familiar without them actually meeting.

The first real meeting needs to be controlled – the worst thing that can happen is that one cat chases the other and violence occurs. This is where the cage or pen comes in. With the new cat or kitten inside it, the resident cat can put the scent and the sight together and investigate, but safely. You could move the cage into a room where you spend a lot of time, such as the kitchen or sitting room, so that it's at the heart of the household but still safe. Hopefully after some initial spitting and hissing the resident cat will get over its initial shock and begin to see the new cat, like its smell, as a normal part of life and the household.

Keep mixing scents and thinking cat. Gradually, when things are calm and quiet and perhaps you're watching television and the room is warm and cosy, start to have the new cat present outside of its cage. Make sure both cats have somewhere to escape to (high-up places are good), and reward them both for being calm and in the same

sharpening and the scent from its paws. Your home is well and truly possessed by your cat.

What you have to try to do is work in the scent of the new cat so that it, too, is incorporated into the accepted household aroma. This comes down initially to you. You have to try and spread and mix the scents of the cats. You're working with the invisible, but have faith that there's actually something there! Put the new cat or kitten into a room of its own, preferably giving it a dog pen or kittening pen or a large cage as a den in which you can put its bed and which you can use a little further down the line during your introductions. If you haven't got one, then at least make sure you have a cat carrier that you can use later on.

room. You want your resident cat and the new cat to associate good things with each other's presence.

Be careful when you go out to make sure that nothing bad can happen – if that means separating the cats then that's fine. One bad encounter can set you back a long way.

How successful you are will depend on several things, not least whether your resident cat is willing to accept a new cat at all – some will, some won't – and whether the new cat is willing to be accepted. However, by gradually integrating the newcomer into the house you're giving them both the best possible chance. Some cats will be snuggling up together after a couple of days and seem to become friends, but the best you can hope for with others is that they'll live peacefully in the same house but very much apart. Review the situation as you go along. These things can take months,

so don't give up immediately. If you're going to let the new cat go outside after a couple of weeks, then this will give them more space in which to manoeuvre.

It's usually easier to introduce a new kitten than an adult cat – somehow this is less threatening. Perhaps it's because kittens don't give off adult smells, or there may be some type of scent that makes them more acceptable, or perhaps their body language and movements aren't so threatening. A kitten is probably more malleable too, and will fit in with the resident cat because it doesn't know much different and isn't in itself defensive, as it hasn't yet taken on the concept of territoriality and hasn't been through the mill of being threatened by strange cats outdoors. However, millions of cats have been successfully introduced into homes with other cats, so it can and does work.

How many cats can I have living in my house?

It's very easy to 'collect' cats – they're addictively beautiful, they're small and they're quite easy to care for. Even if they don't get on they tend to remove themselves from the situation rather than fight. However, there may be a great deal of tension there which owners just don't pick up on. They may start to spray or soil in the house because they're trying to deal with a situation where they feel under stress, and this might be all that owners notice.

If you have two cats living together very successfully then think very carefully before you add more. If you have

three cats living well together then thank your stars and quit while you're ahead! The trouble with adding more is that it might not be just the relationship between the resident cats and the new one that causes problems; it may upset the whole equilibrium of the resident cats' relationship and introduce difficulties between them as tension and stress levels rise.

The best way to have two cats that get on is to get siblings. These will have grown up together, and this usually bodes well for a good future relationship.

How do you introduce a cat to a dog?

Traditionally we think of dogs and cats as enemies (probably from watching too many Tom and Jerry cartoons). However, while they may be wary of each other initially as unknown entities, they can and often do get on very well. Indeed, because there's no direct competition a cat and a dog may get on a great deal better than two cats.

Success in introducing them to one another will depend on several things, including the dog's breed, its age and how well controlled it is. Very close relationships between dogs and cats are usually a result of good early experience and socialisation in both species, but can be achieved by a careful and patient introduction.

If the dog or cat has lived with the other species before this will help the process, as they'll probably be much less stressed by the mere presence of another creature. If the dog has lived with a cat before it may initially show interest in the new individual but will probably soon settle back into doing what the cat tells it to, just like it did before! However, if you're unsure how your dog will react then you need to take care. Be particularly aware that if you have a terrier or a chasing breed such as a greyhound it may be much more driven by its instincts to chase than other types.

- Introduce the dog and cat to each other either with the cat in a kittening pen or the dog in a dog pen. This will ensure that no chasing ensues, no matter what.
- Tire the dog out first by taking it for a long walk, so that it's not so excitable when it comes to meeting the cat.
- Stroke both animals and exchange scents so that they're at least familiar with each other's smell and it becomes a component of the household smell – that of their den.
- Let the dog sniff the cat through the cage. The cat may hiss and growl, but it's safe. The dog may also be wary of this display and grateful that the cat is inside!
- Reward the dog for quiet interaction and the behaviour you want.
- Bring the cage into the sitting room in the evening and all sit quietly watching the television so that no great interest is taken in either animal and it all feels very relaxed and normal.
- If the kitchen is big enough you can put the cage in there during the first week or two and let the dog wander

around while the cat is inside – they'll soon become used to each other.
- The first time they meet outside the cage make sure that the dog is on a lead and can't follow if the cat runs away.
- Make sure the cat has lots of high places to escape to – shelves, window sills, etc.
- Never leave the dog and cat alone together until you're happy that they're safe together.

THE RIGHT CAT FOR YOU

What do you want or expect from a cat?

If you're thinking of getting a cat it's worth considering what it is you're actually looking for. Do you want to be able to handle it, pick it up, have it interact with your family and friends, or do you simply want a cat to be around your home and enjoy its independent presence without necessarily being able to touch or cuddle it?

Many of us simply inherit a cat, or it moves in after hanging around in the garden and looking at us with pleading eyes. After a pathetic miaow or two we give it a bit of food and invite it in – just into the kitchen, of course. Next thing we know it's curled up on the end of the bed and we're running around finding the food it prefers and keeping the heating on to make sure it's warm! Often, in this way, we don't get to actually choose the cat, it chooses us, and we accept the character we get – be it demanding, nervous, friendly or even quite untouchable – and adapt our relationship with it to suit.

However, sometimes we do actually go to a breeder or a rescue centre and have a choice of cats. So how do we select? This is where you need to think about what you want from your relationship with a cat. If you're the kind of person who really needs to have a close relationship with your cat and be able to handle it and have it interact with

you, then you'll be disappointed if you take on a nervous cat that hides every time you come into the room. While there's no guaranteed way to choose the perfect cat, there are things you can look out for. If you understand what makes cats tick, this can help you to bring home a cat which should be able to cope with what you want, your household and your lifestyle.

Think about the different kinds of home a cat could be brought back to, from an old lady who rarely has visitors and leads a very quiet life, to a household with kids ranging from five to fifteen, dogs, other cats, friends visiting, kids playing Guitar Hero or Wii sports, strange bikes and clothes left around the house, people coming and going, phones ringing, and dogs barking whenever the doorbell rings. There are many cats that would live very happily in the midst of the second scenario, even thriving on interactions with all of the different people.

But there are some cats (and probably quite a lot of people) for whom this would be an absolute nightmare, and they'd be stressed up with fear because they'd find it difficult to cope with so many changes in their lives. Some cats need to know exactly what's going to happen when, and these would obviously not fit well into the second household. Such a cat might, however, be very happy indeed with the predictable and quiet old lady, who makes very few demands and is happy to sit quietly until the cat feels confident enough to creep on to her lap. So how to do you tell one cat from another in terms of their ability to cope, and why is it that some cats are people cats and others aren't?

What makes a cat a 'people cat'?

The cats we come across in our lives can vary from pet cat to feral cat. A pet cat could be defined as one that's happy to be around people and to interact with them. Within this group there are a variety of cat personalities that are explored below. However, at the other end of the spectrum is the feral cat, an amazing creature which, although it looks exactly the same as a pet cat and is of the same species, can behave very differently – in fact more like a cat belonging to a wild species.

Feral cats

So what is a feral cat? It's cat born in the wild and never handled, living a solitary lifestyle or within a colony of feral

Left: Feral cats can live in groups but will be wary of people.

cats. Once mature, it regards all people as hazards, although, rarely, it may come to trust food-providing individuals and even allow itself to be touched. It's most unlikely to establish any closer social acceptance of people.

It's possible to turn a feral kitten into a pet if it's handled at a very young age, between two and eight weeks, though it's best to bring it into a human home and handle it before it's five weeks old – in other words before it begins to fear things around it and learns to avoid situations and people. A feral kitten becomes ever more difficult to tame after weaning, and taming is virtually impossible after the onset of sexual maturation.

Stray cats

What we think of as a stray cat is one that was born and raised with people but is now living rough and fending for itself. It retains the capacity to form friendly social bonds with people, though it becomes ever more wary the longer it spends as a stray. A stray may join a feral group and behave similarly reactively and remain shy of people. But unlike the wild-born, unhandled feral cat, a stray will relax and accept handling if caught and will readily establish social relations with new owners and become a pet again.

Pet cats

Within what we think of as the 'pet cat group' can be found a wide range of cat personalities, which are developed for the most part in kittenhood. Much of this personality development has already taken place before we

get our cats and even before we get our kittens. For the cat, learning to enjoy the company of people takes place pretty early in its life – somewhere from about three weeks to seven or eight weeks old. During this time the kitten hasn't yet learned to fear everything, and its mind is open to forming bonds with other animals or people and to learning how to deal with new experiences without being overwhelmed by them. Think about human children when they're toddlers, and how fearless they often are – running off without a care, touching and tasting everything, falling over and getting up again. But as they get older they begin to worry and look for reassurance when they do things.

Left: Stray cats can live in a wild manner but can adapt back to living with people.

51

If kittens don't experience people or human things during the early weeks of their lives they may never be able to see them as part of 'normal' life. Whatever happens in the feline mind as it matures in the first couple of months, it learns to avoid and fear things that aren't familiar to it and this then seems to be fairly fixed thereafter. So a kitten which hasn't been handled by people, met dogs or experienced everyday things such as vacuum cleaners, doorbells, children laughing and screaming and so on will automatically find them very threatening and react accordingly. It will try to avoid any interaction, perhaps hiding away or being aggressive if it's pursued to be stroked. People think that they're being kind in trying to nurture or 'tame' such cats, but often all they're doing is causing great stress. The cat's mind doesn't really have the ability to respond because the pathways weren't created when it was young enough. Cats do continue to learn beyond eight weeks of age, but if the fundamentals are missing there may be little or nothing to build upon.

Right: Handling young kittens and getting them used to everyday sights and sounds will help them to relax in our homes.

Of course, like people, cats will have a genetic input to how they react to the world. Some will be bold, some naturally nervous or shy. This, added to the need for social interaction at a young age, will help to mould the adult cat you see. Additionally if the cat has had traumatic experiences, such as being treated cruelly or being wounded by a dog, this will impact on how it deals with

Personality is a combination of genetics, early experiences and life experience.

doors or lots of visitors, a rather less robust character may suit perfectly. If you want a cat that lives outdoors most of the time and simply want to respect it as a cat, appreciate its mousing activities and feed and care for it at a distance it's comfortable with, then there are some less people-orientated cats which will be very happy to live this type of life.

When we think about getting a cat most of us automatically go for the most obvious thing, coat colour and pattern. Ask anyone who works in a rescue organisation and they'll tell you that the gingers and the tabbies are usually chosen first while the black and black-and-white cats take longer to home. Cats are creatures of

the world. In order to survive in a dangerous world, cats must learn about their environment. They do this as we do, through fear, frustration, pleasure and the other emotions we're familiar with.

Cats are very fast learners and fast reactors – they need to be to survive. If you're a fearful cat and you run away from any interaction with people you'll survive, and you won't question that instinct – indeed, your survival is proof that you were right to keep out of the way in the first place! So a fearful cat will always be reacting a lot quicker than you and won't recognise or realise that you're trying to make it feel different. This can be the problem when trying to alter the character of a cat – if the basic trust isn't there it can be very difficult. However, if you take a cat that's had a good relationship with people but for some reason has been living wild, it may revert to being a pet quite readily, especially as it will already know that there are benefits to having a human carer.

So, what's the point of this discussion about cat personality? It's to try and help you to choose a cat that will live with you so that you enjoy it and it enjoys you. If you choose a fearful cat because you feel sorry for it, and think that just by being kind you'll bring it around, you may have a long and disappointing relationship. The cat may actually be very stressed, because you're asking it to live in a household that holds many fearful challenges for it. On the other hand if you live a very quiet life and want a cat that's not too demanding and will gradually get used to you and won't be challenged by noisy teenagers or loud music, banging

Above: Gingers are always popular.

Right: Black and whites may not be chosen first but are all beautiful!

great beauty and we can't be blamed for being attracted to the most exotic or interesting fur. However, over what might be the 20 years that a cat might live with us, even the most battered and war-torn old tom can work his way into our hearts. Beauty in cats is definitely skin-deep, but their strength of character and appeal is a lot deeper. And anyway, all cats are beautiful!

Many people automatically assume they want to take on a kitten if they're getting a new cat, but there are pros and cons to this and it's worth considering whether you could or would actually do better to take on an adult cat that needs a home. So, what are these pros and cons?

The kitten option

■ A kitten gives you the opportunity to take on an animal right from the beginning and treat it and care for it so that it gets the best start in life.

■ You can get a good idea of its character, but obviously not a full one.

■ If the kitten is a moggie and its parentage is unknown (at least on the paternal side) it may develop a longer coat than you desire.

■ Kittens are like small children – you forget what hard work they are! They require attention to detail and some preventative forethought so that they don't get themselves into trouble.

■ Kittens are likely to have lots of moments of madness and will also climb the curtains!

- If you leave them alone you have to make sure they're safe.
- A kitten is probably easier to introduce to a resident cat than an adult cat would be.
- A kitten is more likely to find a home than an adult cat.
- Kittens have a huge 'cute' factor but they don't stay kittens for very long – just six months out of a potential 14 years or more.
- You may have to organise neutering, initial vaccinations and so on, depending on where you get your kitten from.

The adult cat option

- What you see is what you get – you have more opportunity to see the formed character of the cat, as long as you've viewed it in conditions where it feels comfortable and relaxed.
- It's likely to move in and settle very quickly. It will be much easier to leave it alone in the knowledge that it's not going to get itself into trouble, and it will generally be much less hard work and worry than a kitten.
- There are many fantastic adult cats which needs homes and don't get the chance because people only consider a kitten.
- An adult cat will probably already be neutered and vaccinated.

Which sex?

Whether you choose a male or female kitten probably doesn't make that much difference, as long as you neuter it early enough to prevent the commencement of reproductive behaviour when it reaches puberty. This, of course, is very different for male and female cats, and many of the differences between the sexes are controlled by the hormones that dominate a cat's reproductive life. Un-neutered mature males will mark their territory with very strong-smelling urine, will fight and will roam for many miles in search of females to mate with. Un-neutered females will come into season every two weeks if they don't become pregnant (see Chapter 8 for more details of the cat's reproductive life). However, when we neuter kittens before the influence of these sex hormones kicks in we find that there isn't a great deal of difference between the behaviour of males and females, so if you're getting just one cat or kitten then it doesn't really matter which sex you choose.

If you want two kittens and you're getting them from the same litter it probably doesn't matter what combination you go for; however, if you

have a resident cat and are getting just one kitten or another cat then I'd suggest that you go for one of the opposite sex, just to try and remove some of the competition factor. A kitten may also be a better option than another adult cat under these circumstances, as the young cat's immaturity seems to likewise remove the competition factor – for a while anyway, during which time they'll hopefully get to like each other.

As with all things feline, however, each cat is very much an individual and may or may not take to one cat or to another – in the same way that we may not take to an adult or child who's come to live with us, so it is with cats!

What kind of a person are you?

As pets go, cats are relatively low maintenance if they have to be. However, like any pet they do need care, and some need more care than others. Later in this book we shall

look at products and services for cats and how you can assess them (see Chapter 9) But in the meantime, what about *you* – do you want to spend a lot of time with your cat, do you want it to be demanding, are you expecting to be emotionally reliant on it, are you house-proud – or are you even allergic? These factors need to be taken into account when trying to ensure the best 'match' between you and your new cat.

Again it's about expectations. If you're not likely to have the time or inclination to groom a cat on a daily basis then don't even think of getting a Persian, nor even one of the semi-longhaired breeds – those coats may look luxurious and warm and cuddly, but they're very hard work. And bear in mind that many of the cats endowed with these long coats may not actually welcome grooming if their previous experience has been of someone pulling at knots. They may not even appreciate being restrained while you try to keep the coat under control. If you're extremely house-proud you may not want their long hairs everywhere either. And if the cat goes outdoors it may bring in all sorts of things attached to its coat, especially in the summer and autumn when seeds, twigs and even slugs get lodged there.

A shorthaired cat is a much easier option, as most cats are fanatical about their coat and keep it in immaculate condition. That's not to say that they don't leave hairs around, though – bear this in mind if you're thinking of getting a white cat but have dark furniture, or vice versa. Alternatively buy your furniture to go with your cat! It may

try and deal with this (see boxout), but it's best to acknowledge from the outset that your cat is an animal with free will and natural behaviour that may not suit someone who needs to have an immaculate house. Otherwise your relationship may founder on carpet or furniture issues, no matter how lovely the cat is.

This may all sound obvious, but many a cat finds itself in a rescue centre or even at the veterinary surgery to be put down for just such reasons. Just remember that a cat isn't a doll or a fluffy toy. It will sometimes do things we don't expect and won't necessarily be controllable, and in our busy lives we're often somewhat inflexible regarding things that don't do what we think they should.

Are you a vegetarian and expecting your cat to be one too? This is now a not uncommon scenario and one that results from a complete misunderstanding of what a cat is. This is explored in more depth in Chapter 2, but in short, if you want a vegetarian pet which won't challenge your beliefs, then get a rabbit – a cat is a carnivore first and foremost and looks and behaves as it does for just this reason.

You may have a great aversion to your cat hunting outside. Perhaps you're a bird lover, or you're simply unable to deal with small carcases on the floor. Again, this is what a cat is and does. Keeping it indoors may prevent it actually killing anything, but it will still need an outlet for this, its most instinctive behaviour, and not all cats will be happy with an indoor lifestyle. Likewise, if you're simply getting a cat to keep vermin at bay you won't want to find yourself

sound rather petty, but these things can make a difference to some people.

Likewise, a cat's quite likely to do a bit of claw-sharpening indoors, often on the stair carpet, sometimes on the furniture or even on the wallpaper. It may be claw-sharpening or marking its territory or may simply enjoy the sensation of scratching on a particular texture – dragging your claws through embossed wallpaper with lots of thick raised patterns that flake off as you do so is probably very satisfying! Again, however, there are things you can do to

Scratching in the house

What can you do?
The cat is not doing this out of spite or in an attempt to cause destruction on purpose - it may be using the furniture as a scratching post or it may be using scratching as a marking behaviour.

Place a scratching post in front of the damaged area. Gently wipe the cat's paws down the post to leave some scent on it and show the cat what to do. Do this several times when the post is new. You could also try rubbing some catnip extract into it. If you see your cat scratching elsewhere, carry it to the post and encourage it to scratch there instead.

Sometimes it is just the 'fun' of scratching material that is keeping a bored cat amused, so give it another outlet for its energies. Play more and encourage hunting games. If your cat likes raised pattern wallpaper you might just like to try something else such as flat paper or paint. Don't encourage the cat by giving it attention when it is scratching.

If your cat is scratching to try and make itself feel more secure then you can try and

identify causes of stress - other cats coming in, changes to the household etc. This might include closing the cat flap and opening and closing the door for the cat yourself. Give the cat somewhere high to hide and watch the world. Try spreading some of the scent from the cat's face by wiping it with a soft cloth and dabbing it where the cat scratches. It can be useful to try and remove the smell using a solution of a biological washing powder and then scrubbing it with surgical spirit (check this does not remove colour from fabrics).

If you have an aversion to hunting, a cat may not be the best for you!

with one which isn't especially interested in huntin', shootin' and fishin' and prefers being a couch potato.

If you want your new cat to get on with other cats you already have – though this isn't necessarily the case, and assumptions can never be made – you should try to choose one which seems to be sociable, but need to bear in mind that it may not turn out to be. After all, if you were put into a house with strangers and expected to curl up on the settee with them at the end of the first week, you might prove a disappointment too!

Right: Some breeds, such as the Siamese, seek interaction.

Below: A cat may be an excellent companion but it is not an emotional prop.

Filling a gap – the cat is a poor emotional prop

We all live very busy lives these days. We have to work hard every day to pay the bills, and have busy weekends in which we try to catch up with everything that needs to be done at home. At the same time we try to preserve some semblance of a social life, and sometimes we try to bring up children as well. Many people end up being single parents or living on their own – both stressful situations, and perhaps not what they intended or expected.

Cats fit much more easily into these modern lifestyles than dogs. Dogs really need someone to be home all day, to let them in and out and to be around as part of their 'pack'. Cats, on the other hand, are independent, they can be left alone much more easily, and they fit into smaller flats and houses. Many are companions to people who have busy and stressful lifestyles and who need some companionship when they go home to relax.

We have many expectations of our cats; being companions is usually one of them. However, we have to remember that cats aren't like dogs or people. They don't need a social system like we do and can live happily on their own. The upshot of this is that they don't have systems in place that enable them to provide support or

A protein present in feline saliva is the cause of allergic reactions to cats.

collaboration – they won't give up something for you or do something for the good of the pack. So if you start to lean on your cat because you're in need of an emotional prop it may not be able to understand or cope.

Behaviourists are finding that some cats today are referred to them because of 'relationship' issues, as opposed to the usual 'behaviour problems' generally caused by the cats' environment. Such owners may have unrealistic and inconsistent views of their cats and how they feel they should behave. This is often to do with overprotection and forcing attention on them to make sure they're alright, or wanting to cuddle them and not letting them escape. With some interactive breeds, such as Siamese, this may simply make them very reactive and seeking of more interaction, but for others it will mean retreating into their own shell to get away from the attention. At the end of the day cats are just cats, and they can only react and interact as their own behavioural traits let them.

Are you allergic to cats?

Many people think it's the cat's hair that causes us to react to them by sneezing, wheezing or itching. In fact it's a protein or allergen called Fd1, present in feline saliva, which causes the problem. Because cats groom themselves regularly they have saliva all over their coat. This dries on the coat, and when the cat scratches, moves or brushes past things the dust or dander and hairs which contain the allergen are spread about. Cat-lovers who really want to have a cat but are allergic sometimes think that by choosing a breed with less, little or no coat they can avoid the problem. However, as it's saliva that's the issue this is unlikely to help, and although longhaired cats do seem to cause more allergic reactions that's probably only because, having more hair, they're also covered with more allergen.

It's worth trying out different cats to see if they elicit less of a reaction from you. Indeed, in the USA one company was developing cats that were free of Fd1, so were hypoallergenic for allergic cat-lovers. They seemed to be doing this by breeding together cats with naturally low levels of Fd1 rather than by tweaking genes, so perhaps there are cats out there that will be naturally less allergenic to some people. Unfortunately it's a very difficult problem to get around for people who react or who have family members who are allergic.

If you *are* allergic to cats, your ability to live in the same house as one will probably depend very much upon on how severe your allergy is and if you can keep it under control by using inhalers, antihistamines and the like. You'll need to talk to

Long-haired cats may cause more allergic problems because there is more saliva-covered hair.

your doctor about this. You can also do things within the house to keep the level of allergen down. For instance, it's best to have bare floors – tiles and polished wood are easy to keep clean and don't collect dust, which will include feline hairs and dander on which Fd1 will have been deposited as the cat groomed. Keep soft furnishings to a minimum (use blinds instead of curtains, etc), invest in a good vacuum cleaner, keep cats out of your bedroom and maintain a good airflow through the house. If you brush the cat wear a pollen mask to prevent inhalation and make sure there's good ventilation. You could also invest in an air filter, but these can be expensive.

There are also several products available from chemists with which you can wipe your cat, which are supposed to reduce the level of allergen on its coat. The effectiveness of these products probably varies and will also depend on the level of reaction a person suffers. Alternatively you could try washing your cat in distilled water, though this is unlikely to prove one of its favourite pastimes! You could also talk to your doctor about having desensitising injections, although these may not be suitable for everyone.

It is natural for a cat to be cautious of new people.

How do you match your lifestyle to a particular cat?

This is an important question because it will help you to avoid disappointment. If you want a confident family cat or one that's very happy to be stroked and cuddled, then you'll have to make sure you get your cat or kitten from the right place and have the right information to assist you in making your choice.

If you're choosing an adult cat from a rescue centre then you'll get a good chance to see what sort of personality it

has, and how it reacts to and interacts with you.

See the cat on its own, with no other cats around (which may influence its behaviour or make it feel nervous), and sit quietly until it relaxes. Let it come and investigate you and see how it reacts to being touched. Some cats will immediately interact, others will try and hide. Of course, being wary is an important part of survival so a cat can't be blamed for being cautious. However, there's a difference between caution, timidity and outright fear, and this is what you need to gauge. Caution can be overcome with a gentle and quiet approach. Timidity may take longer and may linger throughout the cat's life, but with the right owner it can be overcome to some extent.

Fear of people is another matter and may not be easily overcome. It may have come about through cruelty, but it may also be part of the cat's own innate character, a result of its own early experiences. So gain as much information as possible. The cat may have come to the rescue centre as a stray, in which case the centre won't be able to tell you much. However, it may have been handed in with details of its past history (although it may not all be true or there may be holes in the story). However, it does give you something to go on, as will the experience of the staff who've been looking after the cat and getting to know it.

General health points to look for when choosing a cat or kitten

■ Check for signs of ill-health – runny eyes or nose, dirty ears, a dirty or sore area under the tail which may indicate the cat is suffering from diarrhoea.
■ The cat should look well, with bright eyes, a good coat and ease of movement.

As a litter grows

the kittens should be bright and healthy.

- Ask about the cat's health, whether it's been neutered, vaccinated, wormed, treated for fleas etc, and whether there are any ongoing health issues.
- If it needs ongoing medication, ask to be shown how to give the tablets, eye-drops or ear-drops so that you know what you have to do. (See page 96.)
- Information on what the cat is eating should be available so that you continue to use the same food until the cat has settled in, after which you can gradually change it if you need to or want to.

Breed or moggie?

If you're looking for a particular characteristic or a particular breed then, again, be flexible – the characters of individual cats vary more than the characteristics assigned to different breeds. Yes, there are breed predispositions towards certain behaviours – the vocal behaviour of the Siamese, the friendliness of the Maine Coon, the inquisitiveness of the Rex, the laid-back ease of the Ragdoll – but within these breeds there will also be cats that don't behave in the anticipated way. And within the ranks of the good old moggies there are likewise noisy cats, bold cats, dependent cats and so on. Yes, a certain look can be expected when you have a 'proper' breed, but as I've said before, looks aren't everything, and there are other factors you'll also need to consider, such as traits in health which may be inherited and are extremely important when it comes to choosing a cat.

Over 90 per cent of cats in the UK are what we call moggies. They're the result of a mating which, as far as we're concerned, is probably pretty random (we usually have no idea what the tom which mated with our female even looked like), and we have no control over the colour,

body shape or anything else which the kittens will inherit from their parents.

So only about 10 per cent of cats in the UK are pedigree animals. It's interesting to consider the mindset we have when we use the word 'pedigree'. We make lots of assumptions about it – many people feel that it's a sign that the cat is somehow superior to a non-pedigree or moggie. We probably think it's something 'better' because people pay for a pedigree cat, so it's of greater value.

In order to create a 'pedigree' animal we limit and control the individuals that can mate to those which exhibit certain characteristics that we want to have in that particular breed. This happens in all of our domesticated animals, from cattle to dogs. Much of this selection process was initially undertaken to produce animals that could perform a particular function. Cattle were selected for their ability to produce large volumes or milk or produce large

amounts of beef. Dogs were selected to work with sheep, to retrieve game, to chase and to hunt. Animals that were unhealthy or less successful weren't bred from. This built in some robustness and also gave people the choice of a particular animal for a particular task.

Of course, being human, once we saw the different looks and behaviours of different breeds of dog we started to change them more and more, and soon got to the stage of breeding dogs for the 'look' that we decided we wanted. We began to worship the 'breed standard', the written format that defines what a particular breed of dog should look like, and in the process rather lost sight of whether the dog could still function as a dog.

It's very easy in a cat book to attack dog breeding. However, you have to remember that dog breeding at least started because dogs were working animals, and different dogs were required for different tasks. Cats, of course, never had a task aside from pest control, and the moggie or non-pedigree cat is brilliant at that anyway. Perhaps you could say that another function of cats is companionship, but again, most moggies do this well. Certainly some of the breeds we have these days are perhaps a little less independent and rather more people-orientated than others. But pedigree cats have mostly been developed because we wanted a certain *look* – long hair, short hair, different face shape, different coat pattern and so on.

Some breeds originally developed naturally because a certain group of cats was geographically isolated from others, and so developed certain common features. An example of this would be the tail-less Manx, from the Isle of Man. However, we've now taken matters further by creating our own breeds or taking the naturally occurring breeds and controlling them further.

Is there a problem with this? If you look at such breeding for looks simply from the position of cat welfare, then you may see it rather differently to someone who wants to produce a cat with a certain look or type of behaviour. Are there risks to limiting the number and type of animals that can breed? If you control the number of animals that can

mate to produce kittens, and select animals for a certain look so that you concentrate specific traits to make a defined breed, you run the risk of concentrating other traits too. For instance, if even one has a medical problem that can be inherited, such as a heart condition, then this can become a problem within that entire pool of animals.

Sometimes we're so focused on the 'look' (which is, after all, what most people are buying when they take on a pedigree cat) that we don't give enough weight to the health issues. We all like slightly different things and it's only human nature to try and produce something that's a little bit different. If we can do this without doing any harm, then there's no issue to be taken with it. However, when we follow the 'breed standard' mantra as being the ultimate achievement, not acknowledging what problems might arise in the process, it can and has lead to problems, with extremes of body conformation and health problems which become inherited. There are various known inherited problems in cats, detailed information on which can be

found on the Feline Advisory Bureau's website at www. fabcats.org/breeders/inherited_disorders.

What I'm trying to say is that pedigree is no better than moggie. Choosing a pedigree cat may allow you to guarantee a certain 'look', and sometimes a certain general behaviour, but somebody has had to bring together certain cats to produce these, and there are costs involved in the selection, keeping, healthcare and health management of pedigree animals which are passed on to the buyer. For instance, a good breeder needs an excellent knowledge of cat care and health, an understanding of genetics, good management in terms of hygiene and disease control, and an understanding of the developmental needs of cats in order to produce kittens which will make excellent pets – after all, it's no good producing a visually beautiful animal which is afraid of people. They also require certain 'people skills', in order to find good homes and responsible owners for their kittens. Becoming a good breeder is consequently difficult to achieve and requires a large input of time and

understanding. It's a great responsibility that should not be taken on lightly.

As for pedigree breeds, the following basic advice might help you in making a decision.

Firstly, unlike dogs, most cats are a similar size. Yes, Maine Coons are larger than most and the Singapura is smaller, but there are animals even within these breeds which match the proportions of other cats, so on the whole size is not an issue.

Coat length, however, is. While longhairs (or Persians, as they're also known) may look glamorous, they can't actually deal with their own coats themselves. In my view a cat should be able to keep its own coat clean and mat-free without human intervention, but many people enjoy the

The Persian's long coat needs daily care.

grooming that's required to keep longhairs in good condition. The volume of their hair is achieved by a very thick and long undercoat, which requires daily maintenance by owners. When this isn't provided, many such cats end up with their huge coats becoming matted, and have to be clipped or shorn at the veterinary surgery under sedation. Long coats also require owners to keep an eye on their cat's tail end, because it's difficult to defecate in a litter tray (or anywhere else) if your coat is full and gets in the way, and it may need to be cleaned and tidied.

Persians have also been bred to have very flat faces that differ somewhat from what we think of as a 'normal' cat face, with a prominent nose and jaw. Consequently they often have problems with their teeth and their jaw alignments, which may contribute to their inability to groom themselves properly. Their eyes are also very prominent and may not drain properly into the tear duct, so that the lubrication of the eye may be affected. Often their tears spill out over the face instead, which means that owners may have to wipe their eyes regularly too. So, if you want to take on a Persian you need to be sure you're prepared to do all of this on a daily basis.

Indeed, if you're taking on any cat that requires this level of human intervention you need to make sure that it's of a temperament that will *allow* you to do it, and you'll need to be able to do the work gently, so as to make being handled a pleasure rather than torture for the cat. Many cats don't enjoy grooming if it's not done gently and without pulling, and can become quite grumpy when the brush or comb comes out. Grooming then becomes a daily battle of wills, which is depressing for everyone. See page 84 for more information on grooming.

There are some breeds of cat that have a long coat that's not quite as thick as that of the Persian. These are called semi-longhairs and include breeds such as the Maine Coon, the Birman, the Siberian, the Norwegian Forest Cat, the Turkish Van, the Ragdoll, the Somali and

Giving a cat a flat face may cause breathing difficulties, eyes which do not drain properly and a jaw which may not align.

MAINE COON

BIRMAN

RAGDOLL

SOMALI

SIBERIAN

NORWEGIAN FOREST CAT

TURKISH VAN

BALINESE

the Balinese. These don't have the extremely flat face of the Persian but may still need some help with grooming, especially if they're the type of cat that enjoys going outdoors. The coat often picks up all sorts of things from the garden or the countryside, especially during the autumn when there are all those plant seeds with burrs and hooks hanging about just waiting for a lift to pastures new.

These seeds can soon form the centre of a big 'tat' or knot of fur, and may require cutting out if you don't get to them quickly. However, on the whole a semi-longhair coat is easier to deal with than a Persian and can look very magnificent.

Another group of pedigree breeds are called Orientals, and include the Siamese and other types that are usually

SIAMESE

BLUE POINT SIAMESE

KORAT

OCICAT

ABYSSINIAN

BENGAL

EGYPTIAN MAU

BURMILLA

RUSSIAN BLUE

SINGAPURA

SNOWSHOE

BURMESE

BRITISH SHORTHAIR

EXOTIC

REX

SPHYNX

longer and leaner-looking than the average cat, with short hair and fairly angled faces. They have a reputation for being quite talkative and owner-orientated. Siamese can be particularly interactive, which can be a lot of fun but may also mean that they become very reliant on people and much less able to be independent. They may actually be affected by being left alone. While their coat may be low-maintenance – the cat can deal with it very easily on its own – Orientals like the Siamese may nevertheless demand more attention.

Another group are collectively called Foreign, and include interesting and varied breeds such as the Korat, the Ocicat, the Abyssinian, the Bengal, the Burmilla, the Egyptian Mau, the Russian Blue, the Singapura and the Snowshoe. There are some very beautiful cats in this group and on the whole they don't have conformation issues or coat problems.

There are also many shorthaired breeds, ranging from

the Burmese with its strong personality to the British Shorthair and the Exotic. The Exotic is the exception here, as it has the same flat face as the Persian but without the long heavy coat – indeed, it could be described as a short-haired Persian and may have similar problems with its eyes, which might need to be bathed and wiped. The joy of all of these cats, however, is that they can care for their own coat.

The Rex breeds have been developed from cats with a much more sparse and slightly wavy coat, and are quite interactive. They may have some skin problems and require bathing more than regular short-coated cats.

Taking minimal coats to their extreme is the Sphynx, a cat that looks bald but may have a faint covering of very fine hair. However, for me a cat should have a coat which it can groom, since a large chunk of a cat's time is spent grooming, and the action itself seems to have a

MANX

BENGAL

SAVANNAH

relaxing and reassuring effect on the cat. Like the Rex, the Sphynx may also have skin issues. Most have to be bathed regularly, not least because the secretions that usually cover the coat and keep the cat's hair separated and waterproof collect on the skin instead and can cause problems. Similar fatty deposits may be found around the claws as well. If you want one of these cats, it's worth talking to someone who already has one to find out all the details about skin care. Obviously there are also issues about keeping such cats warm, and they'll probably need to be kept indoors because of cold weather and the strong possibility of sunburn. In addition if kittens play or cats fight the skin isn't protected by any fur and so can be damaged much more easily. Indeed, even grooming can irritate their skin, as a cat's tongue is rough and designed to untangle fur and spread oil along the hair shafts.

Then there's the Manx, a breed which evolved in the geographically isolated Isle of Man from a group of cats with an abnormal gene which resulted in the spine and tail not developing normally, a condition that can be likened to spina bifida in humans. The breed moves with a characteristic hopping motion and has to be bred carefully so that cats with very short tails aren't bred together, as this can lead to kitten fatalities. This breed has been around for a long time and is accepted because of that, but it's time to rethink whether we should really be breeding these cats at all.

Finally, there's currently a fashion for mating domestic and wild cats to create hybrids that take on some of the features of the latter. This started with the breeding of the Bengal from the Asian Leopard Cat and our domestic *Felis catus*. The resulting generations have produced a cat that has indeed become a pet, and a very beautiful one, although behaviourists who've seen more than their fair share of Bengal territorial problems might warn against doing this again. In the USA and now coming to the UK are other hybrid breeds such as the Savannah, a cross between the Caracal and *Felis catus*. However, my own instincts tell me that we should leave well alone and enjoy the cats which we have rather than try to produce more by means of crosses which sound dangerous for the domestic cats involved in the mating, and will produce quite large animals which will presumably need to be kept indoors. We know little about their behaviour, or the frustration they may experience at being kept in such an environment, and quite probably they're bought by people with no idea of their origins or the behaviour issues that may arise. It seems to be a step too far. We can all look at these creatures and agree that they're very beautiful and that it would be lovely to have one to look at, but there's a list of questions to which we don't know the answers and potential problems that we shouldn't ignore.

Where to get your cat

As has already been said, many of us simply become cat owners because the cat chooses us – it turns up on the doorstep or in the garden and gradually works its way into the bedroom. Alternatively it's a kitten from an accidental litter born around the corner that needs a home. But earlier in this chapter we also looked at what you might want from your cat, what might affect its personality, and how you can match what you want to a particular cat.

If a cat hasn't already chosen you, you can get one either from a breeder or from a rescue centre. Many breed clubs also have a welfare officer whose job is to try to rehome pedigree cats that are no longer able to stay with their owners.

Taking on a rescued cat

Although all rescue organisations may mean well, not all do well for cats. In the UK we're lucky to have strong charity support for our animals, and thousands are rescued, saved and rehomed. Many of the organisations involved are highly professional and have taken on board the mental and physical health needs of their cats in the way they're cared for. Sadly, however, in some 'rescues' or 'sanctuaries' cats are still kept in conditions not conducive to their mental or physical wellbeing.

You will have probably gathered from all that's gone before that cats don't necessarily relish the company of other cats. While some may be very sociable, others will be absolutely terrified at being put in a communal run with strangers. Yes, they may not fight, but their behaviour is subdued and you'll find each one sits as far as it can from the others, dotted around wherever they can find a bit of space of their own. Good rescues these days give cats their own accommodation, with a warm sleeping place and a run where they can stretch their legs a bit or have a look at what's going on. Cats that come in together and seem to get on very well (the one doesn't necessarily follow from the other, and many a cat from a 'pair' blossoms when it's separated from its companion) may be kept together, but assumptions are not made.

Cats should be kept apart for health reasons too. The viruses that affect cats are clever little organisms that are very efficient at getting from one host to another. Consequently diseases and parasites are easily passed between cats in close proximity.

If you go to a poor-quality rescue centre and see cats being kept in not very good conditions you're bound to feel sorry for them, and will want to take them away and save them properly. But the problem with this is that you may take on a cat that's been made susceptible to infection by being kept in a stressful situation and has potentially been exposed to lots of diseases. You could take home an animal with all sorts of health problems. This may not only be

Make sure you have asked about health issues and preventive care before deciding to take a cat on.

Kittens should be bright eyed, alert and full of energy!

financially disastrous, but emotionally it can be very stressful too as you try to nurse the cat through illness. Add to this the potential risk of taking disease home to cats you may already have and it pays to go somewhere where proper precautions have been taken to prevent all of this from happening.

In good rescues health and wellbeing are understood and staff assess the cat's behaviour and personality and try to match owner to cat as much as possible. Cats will also be checked carefully for health problems and will ideally be neutered, wormed, de-flead and treated for any conditions that may have been identified. That's not to say you

shouldn't take on a cat with an illness or disability. If the rescue can tell you about it and what the cat's needs will be, and is able to give you a full picture on which to base an informed choice, then you can take it on with full knowledge of what needs to be done. A cat that needs an owner prepared to be more of a carer will be very lucky to find a good home. It all comes down to knowing what you're taking on. Many people who have the necessary time, energy and compassion get a great deal of satisfaction from taking on a cat that needs help.

Cats Protection neuter and re-home many thousands of cats every year.

With any cat or kitten, it's always wise to check the obvious health issues – that it looks well, that its coat is shiny and healthy, its eyes are clear and its nose and ears are clean. Check for signs of diarrhoea and ask about vaccinations, parasite treatment, feeding habits and general health care. Again, a good rescue will do all of this and give you advice not only on the cat's preferences and health but how to settle it in and when to do what next. Most rescues will also ensure that cats and kittens are neutered before they're rehomed. If kittens aren't neutered they'll ask new owners to ensure that this is done.

Buying from a breeder

If you decide you want a pedigree cat there are again a couple of different routes to go down, depending on whether you want an adult or a kitten. As mentioned above, many of the breed clubs have welfare groups that take in and rehome cats of that particular breed. They'll have knowledge of the breed's particular needs (such as daily grooming), so that they can find owners who'll be able to care for them properly.

If you do want a pedigree kitten then you have to choose not only the breed you want, but also a breeder who can provide a kitten that's in the best of health and, equally importantly, that will make a good pet. Most people don't just want a cat that has a certain shape, coat length or colour, they also want one that's confident and well balanced. Although people tend to take it for granted that

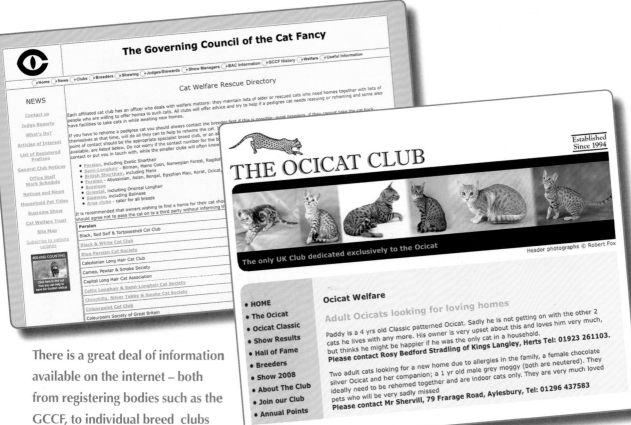

There is a great deal of information available on the internet – both from registering bodies such as the GCCF, to individual breed clubs

lots of handling and care, then they're likely to provide new owners with a healthy, happy kitten. If, however, they're simply trying to make money by producing lots of kittens as quickly as possible without investing the necessary time in their development, then they may well produce fearful kittens. Likewise, having too many cats and kittens crowded together means that those artful cat viruses will have a fantastic playground in which to do their worst.

'Breeder' is not a professional qualification. The description can be used by *anyone* who has accidentally or deliberately bred a litter of kittens, and the quality of breeder varies accordingly. Happily there are breeders who are dedicated to their cats and are very, very knowledgeable, not just about that particular breed but also about cat health and the need for socialisation, and are dedicated to finding excellent homes for the kittens they produce. So the message is *ask questions*, and don't assume that just because a person has a litter of kittens to sell that they know what they're doing and that you'll be getting an animal that's healthy. Read up about the breed and its care, its personality, its needs in terms of attention, its potential for inherited problems, and any tests that can be done to

this comes automatically, that doesn't always happen. As explained on page 51, kittens that don't get the right exposure to people and things human in their first few weeks won't make 'good' pets, or at least, not in the way we expect them to be – confident, gentle and interactive.

There are good breeders and bad breeders. There are those with the knowledge and experience to make their cats' health and welfare their top priority, and there are others who don't really understand cats at all, and don't really care or can't be bothered to do what's necessary to produce a healthy, well-rounded cat. And because a cat's character and reactivity to people are formed almost entirely during the time in which it's with the breeder, this is a heavy responsibility. If the breeder is knowledgeable about cat health, has a small number of breeding cats and ensures that the kittens have

environment, and healthy interactive kittens. If you have a dog then you want to find a breeder that has one too, so that the kittens are used to a canine and accept it as a normal part of life. I would avoid kittens which have been brought up in a shed or outside cattery – they may not have experienced things like the vacuum cleaners, televisions, doorbells, everyday bangs and crashes and visitors that form part of everyday life, and may find them overwhelming.

A good breeder will want to find out if you'll care for the kitten properly and will give you lots of advice on what the kittens are currently eating, the type of litter it's using and what sort of personality it has, so that the move to your home can be made as easy as possible. He or she should be able to provide help or advice if you need it, and will want to hear from you if you have any problems. They should also be willing to take the kitten back should serious problems arise. Both the breeder and the buyer should be confident with each other, and will need to ask questions to establish what level of expertise and experience they each have. Knowledge and information is the key, and ignorance is no excuse for either producing or buying a kitten that's ill or poorly socialised.

Finally, potential owners must be prepared to walk away and not purchase a kitten out of pity because it's ill or scared, just in order to 'save' it from its current environment. Although this sounds very hard, you don't want to be left with a kitten that may have health or attitude problems for years to come and is likely to be difficult and disappointing to live with.

assure you that these problems aren't present in the particular kitten you're interested in.

Do your homework first, and then go and visit. Most breeders will ask you to come along when the kittens are still a bit too young to rehome (the breeding organisations require them to keep kittens until they're about 12 weeks old and have had at least their first vaccinations in order to protect them). Don't go from one breeder to another and handle the kittens – you could carry viruses on your hands and clothes which could be passed on to vulnerable kittens, so breeders may be quite strict about asking you not to do this in order to protect the health of their cats.

Overcrowded, dirty and smelly environments with lots of cats and kittens are not conducive to health or to taking the necessary time to spend with each kitten. If the breeder has a range of litter ages and even breeds to choose from, or has different rooms full of cats, then look elsewhere. What you should be looking for is a home similar to your own, with a healthy-looking mother cat that's confident with people, a clean

FULFILLING YOUR CAT'S NEEDS

What do you need to be a good cat owner?

We've looked at the things you want your cat to be and what personality you're aiming for in trying to match a cat to your lifestyle. However, perhaps you should also be asking the question 'What should I be doing to make sure that I'm the owner my cat needs me to be? What can *I* do?'

Cats don't need a lot in terms of special purchases – food and vet care are really the only things you need to buy specifically. Toys and beds can be made as well as purchased. Usually it's the cat that chooses where it wants to sleep; likewise, you tend to find that its favourite toy is a rolled-up piece of paper, a cardboard box or a paper bag! Just like children, cats definitely prefer playing in the box to playing with the present. Time and interaction are in fact the most valuable commodities, although – again just like children – cats need time to themselves too, to do what they want and to be independent of their owners.

The best way to attend to your cat's wellbeing is to understand it and give it an environment that suits it. Some of the things that make a difference are very simple, but as owners we're actually not often aware of their importance. Sometimes we confuse what cats might want with what *we* might want if we were cats – in other words from a human perspective. Even when you work with information on cats all the time it can still be easy to make assumptions or just not think things through with a feline slant. But as

you start to think like a cat other things will make more sense and you'll start to look at your cat and its reactions in a very different way.

Because cats are very good at hiding their feelings they can be difficult to interpret, and we can make assumptions about quietness, for instance, that are actually 180 degrees wrong. So let's look at some of the ways that better understanding of our cats and what we know about feline behaviour can help them to feel content and remove needless stress from their lives.

Your cat's environment and its importance

One thing we need to realise as owners is that, to cats, more often than not their environment is much more important than the humans that inhabit it. While we may absolutely adore them and feel that our love is enough to keep them happy, our cats can unfortunately be oblivious to this because they're too busy having trouble with the positioning of their litter tray, or feeling unsafe because the neighbour's despotic tom occasionally drops in through the cat flap, eats their food, beats them up and sprays on the door for good measure. Your cat won't be able to relax and enjoy a good cuddle if it's terrified that a rival might be in the heart of its territory and has to keep one ear constantly open for the swing of the cat flap.

We've already seen in Chapter 3 why a cat's territory is

Understanding that your cat does not think like a person will help you understand how to make it feel secure.

Is the despotic tom from next door coming in through your cat flap?

Who's watching who?

so important to it. Though we may think of cats as 'domesticated', we're merely fiddling with millions of years of evolution of a creature that was, in the not too distant past, a solitary animal. Unless you're a lion or part of a related group still under maternal care, then as a cat – large or small – you'd have had to carve out a bit of the landscape big enough to provide you and (if you were female) your kittens with enough wildlife to feed you. Having done this, you don't want another cat around to poach in your larder. So naturally, you're very territorial, because it's a matter of life or death. A wild cat or a feral cat will have a large territory to roam in, a smaller area that it will defend vigorously, and a small den where it feels safe. A female cat will use the den to have her kittens.

Fast forward to the 'den' we call our homes, where we aim to give our cats safety. We think they're safe inside and they may feel that way too. However, we may be unaware of another cat that's visiting through the cat flap or an open window, or looking through the glass windows in the conservatory. Perhaps the next-door cat waits outside the cat flap to pounce on your cat as it emerges. All of these things can make our resident cat feel very threatened and insecure.

If you're aware of the importance of these things you can take measures to ensure your cat actually does feel secure, such as by positioning the litter tray in a safe place and preventing other cats from coming in. This can be done by giving the cat a 'key' on its collar so that it can open its cat flap and other cats can't. This can be done using a magnet or an electronic device, or by installing a cat flap which opens only in response to your cat's existing microchip, which can be programmed into the system.

Have you thought about where you put the food bowl?

What facilities does my cat need?

We all know that a cat needs food and water and, if it stays indoors or is fearful of going out, it needs a litter tray. That's not brain surgery. However, how many of us then line up the food, the water and the litter tray so that they're all close together and convenient for the cat to find and use? And yet you'll find that, given the choice, a cat will drink well away from where it eats and will definitely eat and drink far away from where it goes to the toilet. Convenience is not what it's looking for; rather it appreciates an understanding of the need to separate these important resources.

A kitten will learn very quickly how to use a litter tray.

A litter tray

It's one thing to have the facilities, it's another to be able to get to them and not to feel threatened every time you use them. If you have more than one cat in your household, there may be competition for the food or the litter tray. General advice is to provide one tray per cat, and if you have a number of cats an additional one spare. But the more cats you have the more likely it is that there'll be conflict between some of them.

Trays need to be cleaned our properly by removing the waste every day and washing them out regularly. A tray full of pee and poo won't be an attractive prospect for the fastidious cat and it may start to use other places in the house. Likewise, if you position the tray right where the dog can stick its nose in (or snaffle up the poo) and frighten the cat while it's in this vulnerable position, or where toddlers can get hold of the cat and cuddle it, or where other cats can bully it, then expect it to try and find alternative latrines that are less repulsive to it and make it feel safe enough to squat without feeling too vulnerable.

Think too about the cat's sense of security. You may position the tray somewhere that you think is safe but is in fact in front of glass doors where the cat may feel that the world, and especially other cats, might be able to see in. Some cats may even prefer the privacy of a litter tray with a hood, though others won't like having to get in and out through the small door, which might make them feel more vulnerable. See what seems to suit your cat, and if you have no problems you may well have got it right!

When you buy a litter tray remember that it needs to be quite large so that the cat can get into it and have a scrape around without falling out or scooping all of the litter out.

If you have small kittens or an old cat that's suffering from arthritis you might want to use one with lower sides to make getting in and out a bit easier.

Think too about the litter you choose. There are all sorts of things available these days – litter made from paper, fuller's earth, silica and even corn. Of course, you're the one that has to bring the bulky stuff home, and if you have several cats then you'll be buying and carrying quite a lot of litter. If you talk to behaviourists – who spend a great deal of their time dealing with cats which, for some reason, aren't

Some litters are very fine and sand-like.

using their litter tray but weeing or pooing around the house – they will probably say that cats prefer either fuller's earth or the more sand-like litters, as these are closest to what their ancestors would have used. They might also say that cats with soft feet won't enjoy wood pellets, and that many find perfumed litters very off-putting. Again, it's up to you to find the particular litter that your own cat prefers, or at least a compromise that he'll accept and that's convenient for you to buy and carry home.

If you want to change litters you may want to do this over a couple of clean-outs, since cats like to know what's going on and not to have surprises. If the litter is one thing one day and something completely different the next, the cat may not want to use it or will go looking for what it associates with the litter tray. So if you're going to change, do a bit of mixing to start with so that the cat gets used to the new feel and smell and associates it with going to the toilet.

As I've said, litter trays need to be cleaned out regularly. The theory behind why a cat buries its waste is that probably its scent is thus hidden, and other cats or predators won't know it's in the area. So the idea of doing its business in the same place without the tray being cleaned out, and thereby creating an escalating level of smell, must be very off-putting for a cat. A litter tray is also a great place for organisms to transfer from one cat to another, so while you may pick out the poo and pee as they arrive (if you use a clumping litter), you'll still need to give it a good disinfect every few days or at least weekly. Remember, your cat's sense of smell is very much more sensitive than yours and it will be put off by a stale tray.

Litter tray hygiene is important and should include washing with very hot water and then disinfection using household bleach. Bleach is effective against most viruses and bacteria – dilute one part bleach to 30 parts water. Then rinse and let dry before filling with litter again.

Remember too not to use a disinfectant such as Dettol which turns white when added to water – this usually means that the chemicals involved include phenols, which are toxic to cats.

A cat flap

The cat flap has been the making of cat keeping – it allows the cat free access to the outdoors without having to leave a door or window open, so the house is still secure and the cat doesn't have to live outdoors until it's let in. There are now a wide range of flaps available, simple flaps that are also lockable in or out, flaps that are locked until opened by a magnet or an electronic key on the cat's collar, and recently a cat flap that's triggered by the cat's microchip. Owners can therefore choose to let in all callers, to let in only magnet-wearers, or to be totally specific about which cat can enter by only admitting those whose microchips have been registered with the flap. Having these different facilities is very important, especially if there are other cats in the area that tend to try and visit.

Training a cat to use a litter tray

There are all sorts of litter trays available - some large, some small, some with hoods, some with built in sifting mechanisms. The basics are that you need one which is large enough for the cat to be able to squat and use and to be able to turn around and cover its urine or faeces. The sides need to be high enough to prevent all the litter being scratched over the edge but low enough to allow a small kitten or an older cat to get in easily. Put in enough litter to let the cat dig and cover. Place the tray where the cat can use it easily but not in a busy thoroughfare in the house or where dogs or children can get to it or annoy the cat when it is using it.

We are lucky in that usually, by the time we get our kittens, the mother cat has taught them to use a litter tray. They will naturally dig in soft materials and will automatically use the litter once introduced. Obviously the kitten or cat will have to get used to the position of the litter tray in your home and to any change in litter. It is best initially to use the litter which has been used before just so that the cat/kitten does not have too many things to think about in its new home and some things are familiar and therefore comforting. Once the kitten is using the tray successfully you can change the type of litter gradually if you wish.

Place the kitten on the tray after it has eaten or woken up as this is the time it is most likely to need to use it. If it has an accident then just mop or pick it up with a piece of tissue and place in the tray so the cat associates it as a latrine. Be gentle and consistent and the kitten will soon pick up the habit again.

Prop the cat flap open until the cat learns it is a door.

Encourage the cat to push through and get used to the feel of the door on its back.

The security of a cat's core territory is vitally important to how well it relaxes in its own home, so it's important to make sure that the flap does its job. If you're experiencing an intruder then you need to take steps to keep him out by raising your security level. If the visitor is a complete bully who manages to charge through any flap by means of brute force and determination, then it's better to seal off the flap and simply open the door to let the cat in and out yourself. You may still have to do some rescuing outside if it gets bullied, but at least your own cat will be able to relax indoors secure in the knowledge that the other cat can't get in.

Teaching a kitten to use a cat flap
Once your kitten has had all of its vaccinations you may decide that you want it to go outside and to be able to use the cat flap to do so. If you already have a cat flap and an older cat that already uses the flap you may not have to do anything. Cats learn very quickly by observation, and the kitten will have watched the other cat coming and going out and will have let its curiosity get the better of it. Indeed, if you have a bright, confident kitten you'll probably need to make sure that it doesn't go outside before you're ready!

However, if the cat or kitten hasn't met with a flap before you'll have to show it the basics. Initially the clunk and snap of the flap as it shuts can be rather frightening, as can the door as it touches the cat's back on the way through, with the added fear that its tail will get caught in the flap. Going through is a bit like snorkelling for the first time – the difference between being above water and below water is stark and the world suddenly changes beyond recognition. For a kitten the first exit into the great outdoors is probably pretty scary too.

The best way to get the kitten to investigate is to cut the process into smaller chunks. Prop the door open with a stick or pencil or stick it with tape so that the door is as wide open as possible and won't touch the kitten's back when it goes through. You might want to carry the kitten outside and let it go through the flap in the direction of indoors first, so that it's going into a familiar environment rather than heading into something completely alien. Get someone on the inside to encourage the kitten or cat through and reward it with a treat or toy when it goes through. Then gradually prop the door a little less widely open and let the kitten go through it until it's pushing the door a little and getting used to the sensation. If you want to lock the flap to keep the kitten inside sometimes, put a visual signal there for it, such as a piece of board, so that it's not confused by the flap not budging when it pushes.

A cosy bed
In terms of beds, it's not just the shape, size or fabric that matter, it can often be simply the position of the bed that will either attract or deter a cat from using it. Most of us would instinctively not put a cat's bed on the floor, since we realise that cats feel vulnerable down low, especially if there are other animals or children around, or even just people who clump around in big boots. We know that cats feel better higher up – a high place means that the cat doesn't have to worry about what's above it and can see what's happening below without actually having to get involved. Cats need to have high places within a house to retreat to or just retire to for a safe, quiet nap, or to get out of the way of some household activity or visitor (person or dog). For more nervous cats this can be a godsend – somewhere to relax.

A cat can seek out the softest bed – usually the clean washing basket!

Of course, cats also love beds which allow them to snuggle down and hide. There are igloo-type beds, beds that are a bit like large bags where the sides fold in and cover the cat, baskets, furry beds, and beds that hang on radiators and allow full-on heat absorption. But often the cat's favourite place is our own bed, usually preferred when we're actually in it, providing warmth and protection and conveniently to hand to be prodded when food is required in the morning.

More nervous cats will like to snuggle under something. In times of stress, a cat out of its own environment will try to hide underneath things. You can see this when cats have to go to the vet for an operation or a test. They'll sit in the litter tray and keep very low so as not to be noticed, or will try to hide under the bedding or paper or the fleece lining the cage.

Designer chairs for some!

Recovery beds

Although vets at the Feline Advisory Bureau are funded to specialise in cat medicine, they're not just interested in the complicated treatment of disease, but also in investigating ways of promoting healing and wellbeing, since being in a veterinary hospital situation can make cats feel very stressed. They've found that by giving their patients beds in their recovery cages that are soft and like a large bag that folds in over itself, hiding and protecting the cat, the cats relax more, begin to eat sooner and heal much more quickly. The cats can also be lifted out of their cages in these beds so that there's no struggle when handling them, and often they can stay inside the bed while their temperature is taken or a wound is checked. This is so much less stressful for cats and is part of what the charity calls 'cat-friendly practice'. Great strides have been made in cat care through the observation and application of such simple principles that make cats feel more secure and less stressed.

The same principles can be applied at home for nervous cats, so help them find somewhere to relax. Many cats do this for themselves by snuggling down under the duvet – which is safe enough until someone doesn't realise the small bump on the bed is the cat and sits on it!

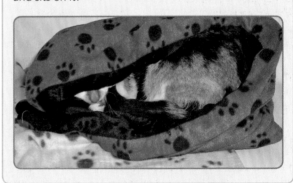

Some cats like to hide away when they sleep.

Grooming your cat

For shorthaired cats or kittens, grooming help from humans isn't essential – it may be something you want to do, or the cat may enjoy the attention, but it's not vital to its wellbeing. However, if you've taken on a longhaired or semi-longhaired cat then it's essential to groom it regularly (daily) in order to keep its thick coat free from mats and tangles.

As with many other things mentioned in this book, it's best to start grooming in kittenhood, even if the coat isn't yet long, so that the cat accepts it as being a normal part of life.

- Use a wide-toothed comb or a brush and gently groom the coat in the same direction as the hair lies.
- Give a treat and praise the cat for allowing you to groom it. Many cats will actively enjoy the sensation.
- If you hit a tangle approach it from the top rather than by pulling the comb through from the hair roots. Gradually loosen the hair and work through it. If need be hold the hair near the skin as you do this so that you avoid pulling it.

- If the knot can't be untangled and combed through then carefully snip it out, using round-nosed scissors to ensure that you don't stab the cat in the process!
- Make grooming sessions short and enjoyable and always stop before the cat gets annoyed.
- Gradually step up the time you spend grooming.
- At she same time as you groom, run your hands over the cat to check for lumps, bumps or parasites such as ticks.

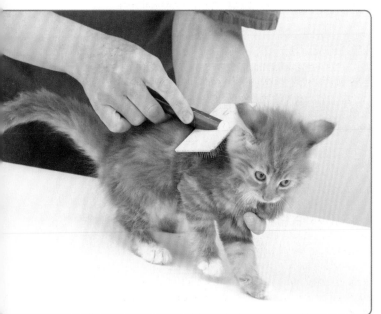

- If you groom a longhaired cat every day you won't have to undertake mass tat removal. This will prevent grooming becoming an unenjoyable ordeal for either you or your cat.
- If the cat really doesn't want you to groom it, try distracting it with a small piece of ham or a favourite titbit and just do a little bit while it's eating – this may call for a lot of patience and a lot of bribes, but it can provide sufficient motivation to persuade your cat to put up with being groomed.
- The places where a cat most dislikes being groomed are under its tummy and around its tail, so do these last if possible.

Removing toxic substances from a cat's coat

Cats hate their coats to be disturbed or dirty. They're so driven to keep them clean and lying flat that they'll even groom off substances which are poisonous and which they'd never ingest voluntarily any other way. These toxic substances include things such as creosote, tar, white spirit and other decorating products. If you find these on your cat's coat or feet, prevent it from grooming and wash them off with a solution of washing up liquid. Don't attempt to use other solvents or cleaning products, which may themselves be toxic to cats. If in doubt contact your vet.

- If you've taken on a longhaired cat that's in really poor condition and won't let you groom it, ask your vet to shave off the coat and start again. Then use a very gentle brush even when the coat is still very short, in order to make grooming a pleasurable experience for the cat. This way you can prevent tats forming as the new hair comes though, and by the time its coat has regrown the cat may have come to trust you not to hurt it and learned that grooming can be enjoyable. Again, great patience is required.

Other cleaning issues

If you have a very flat-faced Persian-type cat it may well have eyes which water constantly and will need wiping on a regular basis. To do this, gently wipe round them with a cotton wool ball dampened with clean water or a little baby oil. Use a separate ball for each eye and dry with a soft tissue. Don't touch the eyeball itself, as this will be painful and the cat will try to avoid the experience next time.

If you think your cat's ears are grubby you might be temped to try cleaning them out with a cotton wool bud. However, most vets would advise you to not to tamper with a cat's ears at all, as the tissues lining its ear canals are very delicate and easily damaged. The ears may be dirty simply because of wax, but it may also be as a result of ear mites or a skin irritation. Check with your vet, who may give you a product to wipe the outer ear – but you must avoid wiping too deep into the ear and causing more damage.

For details on teeth cleaning, see page 113.

Does my cat need to go outside?

Often when people buy a pedigree cat they're told not to let it go outside. That's because 'outside' is perceived to be of high risk to cats. Certainly there are plenty of dangers for a small animal – the car being the primary one. Whether pedigree cats are stolen because they're perceived to be valuable or taken in by someone else because they're attractive is debatable, but the perceived threat is always a good reason to keep them indoors. Many people do keep their cats in and some cats choose not to go outside anyway because they find it too stressful if they're of a nervous disposition, or if they're old and infirm.

However, many other people feel that a cat should be able to go outside if it needs to. There's a huge part of a cat's life that we're unaware of, where it uses all its senses and talents that have evolved over millions of years and behaves as all its instincts tell it to. It can hunt, patrol its territory, mark, sunbathe and generally indulge all the behaviours naturally programmed into its body. Inside our homes the cat is really a shadow of its potential self, with its engine and navigation system and weapons switched off. Outside it comes to life and sharpens up its talents and its body by hunting, climbing, exploring and so on.

Given that a cat which has to hunt to feed itself would need to eat about ten mice a day, and that each actual catch might require three hunts, you can see that a 'normal' cat would spend a lot of its day actively seeking food. It would also need to make sure that its coat is clean and well groomed so that it's sensitive to touch, is waterproof, and doesn't carry a heavy smell that might give it away. That dedication to achieving a perfect coat takes a long time, and for the rest of the time the cat probably sleeps. Thus an active normal cat won't sleep all of the time

in the same way as it's able to do when stuck at home and given everything it needs.

So, there's disagreement when it comes to keeping cats indoors – safety versus natural behaviour. However, there is agreement that if a cat has to stay indoors – whether because it's too nervous to go out, because it's in a genuinely very dangerous place or because its owner can't bear to have it put at any risk at all – then owners need to work hard to compensate for the lack of the stimulation it would get outside.

Should cats go out at night?

The consensus view among animal welfare organisations these days is to try and keep your cat indoors during the evening and night because there's a greater risk of harm at such times. Drivers can't see cats on the road, there may be the risk of encounters with other animals, such as foxes, and to us the night is always full of danger – primarily, of course, because we can't see well in the dark.

Whether there actually *is* a threat from foxes is hard to ascertain. There are stories of cats and foxes playing together; there are tales of cat bones found in fox dens. I suspect that it all depends on the desperation of the fox and the size of the cat. A vixen with cubs to feed in an area where there may not be much food but where there's an abundance of cats may, indeed, feel the need to take on a small cat or kitten. Cats and foxes may also

be competing for the same prey. Where there's plenty of food then they may well live quite happily together. A fox would need to be pretty brave to take on a cat anyway – it's going to fight back and could cause life-threatening injury even to a fox. So I suppose the answer is – it depends...but it's presumably safer to keep the cat in.

If you've trained your cat to expect to be inside at night, and it's used to that routine from the beginning, you should have no problem. However, if you have an active outdoor cat which is used to coming and going as it likes, day or night, you may have difficulty in getting it used to being kept in. It may be stressed when you try, especially if it's spring or summer, when outside is very exciting and not too cold. If it doesn't settle into staying indoors you may simply have to accept the risks and let it out.

Keeping the indoor cat active and alert

A cat which is kept permanently indoors may be at less risk than cats which go out, but the possibility of a long and rather boring life may lie ahead unless its owners make a

Cats need to be active to keep mind and body stimulated.

great deal of effort. If a cat goes out it doesn't need lots of stimulation indoors – it goes out for exercise, adventure, to satiate its curiosity, to follow its hunting or patrolling instincts or just to sunbathe and get some fresh air. Even just going outside to use the garden as a toilet may lead to adventures.

Cats that go out may do a little hunting, which even if they fail to catch anything exercises their bodies and their senses. Behaviourists suggest that an indoor cat shouldn't get anything simply presented to it in a bowl, but should have to work with its brain and its body to get its meals. Owners can buy various products that the cat can chase around and which release food as the cat plays.

Alternatively they can be creative on their own, hiding food around the house, building structures with food inside using *Blue Peter* materials such as cereal packets, egg boxes and toilet-roll tubes. Play 'chase and

Kittens are curious – hiding dry food can be a great game.

retrieve' with dry food, make the cat climb the stairs or jump up on to the windowsill so that it works for its meals.

You could encourage your cat to climb using a cat aerobic centre, either purchased (there are lots to choose from) or of your own construction manufactured from boxes and tubes. Provide a sturdy, good-quality scratching post that's tall and rigid so that the cat can really stretch up and pull down with its claws. Some cats also like horizontal scratching surfaces – see what your own cat prefers.

Many of the cases of cat poisoning seen by vets occur in animals that have no access to outdoors and so don't have natural grasses or herbs to nibble on. Cats need very little plant material in their diet but they do chew some greenery for reasons we're not sure of but may be to do with digestion or self-medication for things such as hairballs. If cats don't have access to outside plants they may nibble instead on those that are available and end up eating poisonous houseplants or bouquets. Owners of indoor cats consequently need to take much more care about the plants their pets have access to. Providing pots of grass or herbs to nibble will provide indoor cats with an alternative that's not dangerous for them.

Young cats that don't go out may also get themselves into all sorts of trouble as they explore the house. Again, owners must be vigilant about what they leave lying around or what machines they leave open that a cat can climb into.

Household hazards

The saying 'curiosity killed the cat' derives from the fact that cats can all too easily get themselves into situations that are dangerous to them. There's very little in our homes that's dangerous to a mature, sensible adult cat, but kittens are more inquisitive, far less sensible and able to get into even smaller spaces, so you do need to be fully aware of potential household hazards if you take on one of these little creatures. Think toddler and you'll be applying the right level of care and attention that's needed when looking after a young kitten. Watch out in particular for:

■ Open washing machines or tumble dryers, which can be very appealing to a small cat, especially when warm. Always check inside before using.
■ Hot hobs. Make sure that kittens can't jump directly up on to them.
■ Pot plants and cut flowers in vases – prevent kittens from nibbling them.
■ Shredders with paper going through, which might be attractive because of the movement.
■ Toxic paint strippers and other decorating materials, which might be spilled or stepped on to or into by an excited kitten.

A cat will need a scratch post which may be an aerobic centre for a kitten!

A Christmas tree will be fascinating but potentially dangerous for a young cat.

- Small holes or gaps through which a kitten can squeeze and get stuck.
- An open chimney that a kitten can climb up and get stuck.
- Needles with thread can get swallowed and thread can get wound around a cat's tongue.
- Ironing boards and hot irons – a rickety ironing board may not support a kitten climbing on to it.
- Wires that can be pulled or chewed – both potentially dangerous!

Christmas trees and hanging baubles are almost irresistible to many cats, especially young ones, who are likely either to play with the moving decorations or climb up inside for the sheer fun of it! Tinsel, mistletoe, holly and other small pieces can be especially hazardous to a curious cat.

If you have children who like to jump on the cushions and furniture, warn them that a small kitten or cat may be asleep underneath!

Does a cat need a friend?

When cats started to live around humans because of the availability of prey in their grain stores and habitations, the individuals that were able to overcome their fears of man and learned to be around other cats were the ones that ate well and produced healthy kittens. These more tolerant cats had an advantage and learned to live in groups if there was enough food. Those that lived closely together were in related groups where there was a survival reward for tolerating or even helping related offspring. Strange cats were not welcome.

Most of this instinct remains strongly intact in our pet cats today. The natural reaction to a strange cat is to be highly wary of it and to feel threatened. This doesn't mean that you can't add another cat to your home, and many people do so very successfully. What it *does* mean is that if you want to have more than one cat then think about it carefully and approach it from this viewpoint, don't just expect your cat to accept another one without showing any reaction. Acknowledge that it might be you rather than your cat that wants to have another cat around, and make your choice and introduction carefully, as outlined in Chapter 4.

If you already have an indoor cat and you want to introduce another cat then you also need to be aware that this can be much more difficult, as the resident cat's whole territory is being violated – it has no outdoors to retreat to for space and peace. You'll need to take things slowly and carefully. If you know you're going to keep your cat indoors and feel it would be better to have another cat around for stimulation and company, then the easiest way is to get two kittens at the same time or give a home to two cats that are already compatible and are used to staying indoors.

Some cats will accept an addition to the famly, others may not be so tolerant or accepting.

What else does a cat need to do?

We've already discussed the cat's hunting activities, and that if it can't go outside there needs to be an outlet for this activity through play and interaction with its owners. After all, a cat looks like it does and behaves as it does simply because it's a top-of-the-chain predator. If it was vegetarian it would look like a rabbit – form follows function.

Within this 'prime directive' of hunting, the cat has two particular behaviours that are key parts of it keeping itself in prime condition for survival – grooming and claw-sharpening. A cat can groom whether inside or out, so as long as it gets enough time to relax sufficiently to do this – *ie* it isn't hounded by other cats, dogs or children. In fact cats can sometimes take grooming too far. It seems to have several functions beyond cleanliness, including relaxation and the spreading and sharing of scent. Grooming is probably quite a pleasurable experience for cats too – they must get some reward which ensures that they don't just give up on a bad tat and are prepared to groom things off their coats that their natural instincts wouldn't normally let them swallow. Examples would be something like creosote, which is poisonous to cats, or tar products that get stuck to their paws. Grooming must therefore have a very strong drive, perhaps because the cat feels pleasure in doing it. This would also explain why cats like us stroking them (as long as they perceive no threat and they're used to human contact).

As we've already seen, the cat's claws are a fantastic design of lethal weapon for grabbing and holding prey and for self-defence if necessary. At the same time as having these weapons on all of its feet, the cat must also be able to move silently, hence the brilliant adaptation of a retractable or extendable claw that's sheathed in a velvet pouch to prevent it clicking or catching when the cat is walking around or hunting. Instantaneous unsheathing is also required to enable the cat to catch and hold small animals with super-fast reactions of their own. And the tips have to be razor sharp. All of us who've had new knives in our kitchens know that if you don't look after them they become blunt pretty quickly and then aren't much use for anything. But as described earlier, a cat keeps its claws sharp by peeling off the outer layer of nail to reveal a gleaming new point underneath. It does this by pulling its nails through a resistant material – wood and bark work for the outdoor cat, a scratching post, the carpet and the

arms of settees for the indoor cat (and the outdoor cat that likes to do its sharpening indoors or just can't resist the wallpaper in the hall, especially the one with all the raised lumps and flock).

Cats like security

We often think of cats as being the favourite pets of artists and creative types, of being independent and adaptable, not having to be controlled or to fit into any specific type of lifestyle. Indeed, it's the very flexibility of the cat that has made it such a successful pet. However, just because it seems to have a very laid-back lifestyle – sleeping quite a lot, interacting with you, going out when it likes, not having to be taken out for walk before you leave for work or last thing at night like a dog – doesn't mean that the cat doesn't like or need security or structure in its life. Indeed, we often think that because we're there to 'protect' them cats don't have to worry about anything. But that's not the way *they* think. Although they're what we would call 'top-of-the-chain' predators (*ie* they're at the top of the hunting tree), they can themselves become prey to some animals, and because they're small can be severely injured by dogs and other cats or animals they may encounter.

The most relaxed cats are either the very confident ones who feel that they can cope with changes or challenges as they occur, or cats that know what's happening in their

lives. Security can mean knowing that other cats won't be entering their den (your house), or beating them up every time they go outside. It can also mean knowing what's going to happen when – how the household ticks along, when they'll be fed, and so on. Cats feel secure if they don't have too many surprises. The more unsure the cat is of itself and its environment, the more it will appreciate knowing what's going to happen next; then it doesn't have to worry. So some cats like routine, and it's a tool that

Blink rather than stare at your cat as staring is regarded as a challenge by a cat.

owners can use to make them feel more secure and relaxed. It's another case of trying to get inside the cat's head to understand what's important in its world rather than seeing things from a purely human perspective and expecting the cat to behave accordingly.

So, having said that cats like to feel secure, what sort of things do they find threatening? Again, this will vary from cat to cat. In general cats don't like unknown cats on their territory, and will hide or run from things which are strange and loud and encroach upon them. Some will feel threatened simply by an unknown person coming into the house or the doorbell ringing, while others can live in a completely chaotic house and not turn a whisker.

If a cat feels threatened its usual reaction is to remove itself from the situation, to make itself small and quiet and hope it isn't noticed. If threatened further it will try to look bigger than it is by fluffing up its fur and standing sideways. It will try and position itself so that it can run away without providing a vulnerable target, or it may assume a defensive posture in case it's attacked.

It's all about knowing your own cat – observing its body language, seeing what it likes and doesn't like, what it responds to and what can send it into a spin. Think about what a cat would do in the wild and try to understand the equivalent experience of your own cat within its domesticated circumstances.

Making friends with your cat

- Approach your cat in a non-threatening way, quietly and slowly.
- Blink rather than stare, as staring is regarded as a challenge by cats.
- Stick to stroking areas that the cat is relaxed about you touching – probably the head and along the back at first.
- Avoid tickling its tummy and other areas about which the cat may feel defensive.
- Avoid holding its paws or fiddling with its tail.
- If the cat wants to move away from you, let it go and return later.
- Keep interactive sessions short and pleasant if the cat is worried or unsure.
- Find out which food your cat really likes and use it to encourage interaction.
- Play with your cat and see which games it prefers – use these to encourage it to spend time with you.

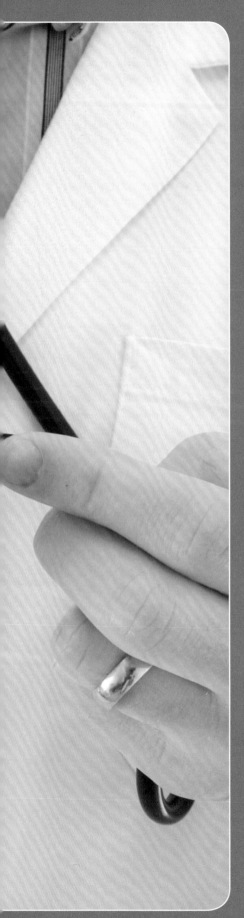

KEEPING YOUR CAT HEALTHY

Cats are not small dogs

Anyone who's familiar with the behaviour of the cat will know that the saying 'a cat is not a small dog' is indeed very true. Apply it to the *health* of a cat and you have a statement that's not only true but also contains a hint of a warning: you can't just take the diagnoses and treatments applicable to dogs and scale them down to a cat.

The cat, of course, has its own unique physiology, diseases and reactions to drugs and treatments. The treatment of illnesses in the dog was developed much earlier in veterinary history than for the cat, because the dog was a valued working animal which had a job to do. Consequently cat-lovers and vets interested in felines had to develop feline medicine anew in the early 1960s.

In addition to having a different physiology to dogs, cats also have their own set of behaviours that can make even noticing illness very difficult. Cats never make things straightforward, which is probably why so many of us are fascinated by them – you need to be a good detective to work out a cat! So what are the extra hurdles which cats present when it comes to their health?

Masters of disguise

It's remarkably difficult to age a cat just by looking at it. Yes, in its first year, or even its second, the cat has a youthful look and energy that give us some clues. However, after that many of our cats can seem to remain unchanged into their mid-teens if they're lucky. As they get into double figures many dogs go grey around the muzzle and face, move less easily and change their body shape – it's fairly obvious that they're ageing. But the youthful-looking cat doesn't go grey and could easily fool you as to its actual years. If it looks old it's probably *very* old.

Cats look well even when they aren't

Cats are predators and as such we think of them always at the killing end of a predator/prey encounter and always on top. However, as I've pointed out several times the cat is a *small* predator, and there are other animals (and even people) who'd be happy to treat it as prey as well. The cat, of course, is well aware of this. It doesn't have a pack to hide within like a dog, no others of its kind that are going to stand up for it or provide a united front against a threat. It's a small animal with only itself to rely on when it comes to avoiding or escaping from a dangerous situation. Therefore it needs to ensure that it doesn't show vulnerability or weakness that might draw an opportunistic predator's attention.

Probably because of this, cats are masters of disguise when it comes to not revealing that they're ill. They don't whine like the dog. They often just become quiet and stoic, and unless you notice that this is in fact a change in their normal behaviour you may not take a second glance – the

Cats can hide pain remarkably well.

A change in drinking habits can be a sign of illness.

cat removes itself from the radar and merges into the background until it feels better.

When illness does show it's often serious

Cats can hide signs of illness for a long time and many organs can keep going at almost normal rates until they reach a certain point – which, for cats, is often well into the illness. For example, older cats often suffer from kidney disease. The cat's kidney is a fantastic organ that can function pretty normally until about 75 per cent of it becomes affected – then the cat starts to show signs such as drinking more. So diseases in the cat can be quite far advanced when we start to notice them.

As cats age more complex things can go wrong

Though young animals can become ill, they usually suffer from one particular illness at a time, which can be tackled individually. As a cat gets older, however, the chance of an organ or body system going wrong increases, and there's a likelihood that several things may happen at once as the body ages. Once again, therefore, it pays to keep a close eye on your cat.

Watch out for behaviour changes

As mentioned above, cats often just go quiet when they're ill, and in a busy household where the cat uses the garden rather than a litter tray as its toilet there may be no obvious signs that it's unwell. It may be one of those cats that drinks outside because it prefers rainwater to water in a dish, so owners may not even notice an increase in thirst and drinking. Without a litter tray owners may not notice diarrhoea or a change in the volume of urine, and so not pick up these pointers to a problem. If the cat has simply gone quiet or seems to sleep more nobody may ask any questions. If it's less interactive or a bit grumpy it takes an owner who can let this clue enter his or her consciousness in a busy life to realise that it might mean something.

Cats don't like going in the car, let alone to the vet

Cats usually hate being put in the cat basket – they vanish somewhere into the mist even as it comes out of storage. Then you have to put them in the car, where it's usually obvious that they don't enjoy the experience, and after that you have to take them into the vet and deal with the stresses there. So owners don't usually enjoy taking their cat to the vet, and may consequently postpone the struggle until the cat is looking worse. However, there are ways in which the whole experience can be much improved, so don't give up hope – see page 126.

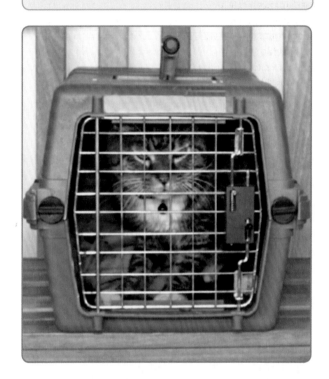

Giving medication to your cat

Cats often don't make it easy for us to care for them. They don't mind it if we handle them for cuddling or stroking, but as soon as we try to restrain them for the purpose of giving them a pill or a potion they seem to instinctively know what's going on and try to get away. Giving a cat a single pill can consequently turn into a major struggle.

Unsurprisingly under such circumstances, it takes a dedicated owner to persist. Often treatments are started and then abandoned, especially if there seems to be a bit of improvement. However, with treatments such as, for example, antibiotics it's important that the whole course is taken so that antibiotic resistance doesn't develop.

Giving your cat a pill

The trouble with treating cats is that they can be very wriggly, are surprisingly strong for their size and, of course, they have some very sharp weapons which, even when deployed in sheer panic, can inflict nasty injuries. So, as always with cats, the only way to succeed is by being calm, firm and gentle.

■ Start by placing your cat on a table, first putting something under its feet which isn't slippery – ideally a towel or mat that it can cling on to it if it wants. You may also want to get someone to help you so that you don't have to struggle with the cat alone, at least until you get used to the procedure.

■ Use your body and arms to contain the cat within a small area – do this gently, almost without it noticing. Put your hands around its shoulders and chest; you can hold the front legs gently between the last two fingers of each hand if you're worried about being scratched.

■ If you have a cat that can squirm and wriggle its way out of your hold, or that you know is likely to scratch you, get a large towel, place the cat on it on the table and wrap the towel around it so that only its head is showing.

■ Have the pill ready between the thumb and forefinger of your right hand (if you're right-handed).

■ To get the cat to open its mouth, place your left hand over its head and your thumb and forefinger on either side of the jaw. You can hold the cat quite firmly like this and control its head.

■ Tilt its head up gently using the fingers of your right hand (the one holding the pill). It will be hard for the cat to keep its jaw clamped shut once its head is pointing upwards.

■ Put the middle finger of your right hand gently between the cat's canine teeth (the ones which look like fangs) and pull the jaw down, opening the mouth.

■ Keeping your finger on the front of the jaw to keep the mouth open, quickly put the pill in at the back of the mouth.

■ Release the cat's head so that it can swallow and return its head to the normal position.

Place your thumb and forefinger either side of the cat's jaw.

Hold the pill as shown, tilt the jaw upwards and gently open the mouth.

Once the pill is inside, release the cat's head so that it can swallow.

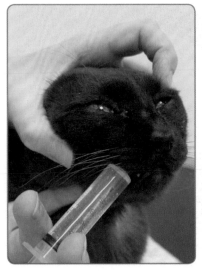

Some tablets can cause damage to the oesophagus (tube down through which food enters the stomach) if they do not move down. Syringing a small amount of water can help – do it gently and slowly.

Obviously, the more practised you are at the procedure and the more swiftly and gently you're able to do it, so that the cat hardly notices, the less of a trauma it will be for all concerned.

If you have real problems giving pills to your cat ask your vet if there are alternatives, or if the pill can be altered to make it easier give to the cat. More and more manufacturers are now making their pills either smaller, more streamlined or even palatable for cats, so that owners don't have to fight with their cats in order to try and help them. The Feline Advisory Bureau actually gives an annual award to companies that have come up with a better method of giving pills or a palatable pill that most cats (it will never be all!) will eat. Though some tablets must be given whole because they have a coating that releases the medication slowly in the stomach, some can be crushed and given on a bit or tuna or in a favourite food, but you need to check with the vet first as some may lose their effectiveness if altered in this way. Others might taste really horrible if they're crushed. Alternatively you may be able to use a gelatine capsule if the tablet is bitter-tasting, but again you need to check with your vet that this doesn't alter the efficacy of the medication.

Some tablets can cause damage if they sit in the cat's windpipe for a period of time, so if possible it's wise to help the medicine go down by syringing a small amount of water into the cat's mouth after the tablet has been taken. You can ask your vet for a syringe. Place it gently between the cat's cheek teeth and dispense a little water slowly so that the cat can swallow it. If this isn't possible you can give your cat a little knob of butter – if he doesn't want to take it directly smear a little bit on his nose so that he licks it off and in swallowing moves the pill down into his stomach.

Finally there are various pill poppers available which you can use to introduce the pill into the cat's mouth and so keep your fingers out of the way. You can ask you vet about these or find them in a pet store. There are some which also introduce water as they give the pill. These are made of strong plastic, so you need to be careful and gentle with them as they could hurt your cat's mouth if forced in.

Giving eye drops or eye ointment

As with other procedures it's probably the restriction to its movement that the cat resists rather than the actual treatment. As with pills, be firm but gentle.

- With the ointment or dropper in your right hand ready to use, place your left hand around the cat's head, over one ear and under the chin. This will clamp one eye shut but leave access to the other one.
- Tilt the cat's head upwards a little and with your thumb and finger pull the eyelids apart.
- Put the drops or a line of the ointment on to the surface of the eye or along the lower eyelid.
- Close the lids and massage gently to spread the medication over the entire eye.
- Repeat for the other eye if necessary.

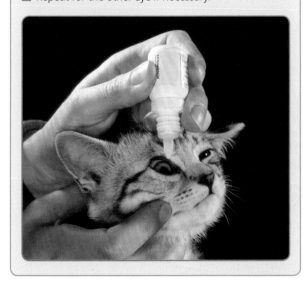

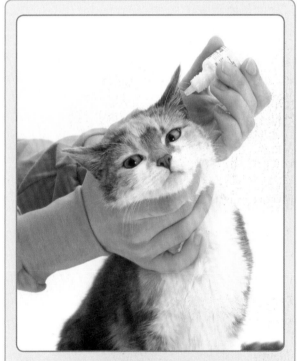

Giving ear drops

- With the bottle ready in the hand which you want to use, hold the cat firmly and gently and tilt its head so that the ear to be medicated is uppermost.
- Quickly squeeze the prescribed number of drops into the ear.
- Hold the flap shut so the cat can't shake it all out again!
- Gently massage the base of the ear to help the medication move down into it.

Giving a 'spot-on' flea or worming preparation

Thankfully many of the medications or treatments we have to give our cats are today available as medicines that can be put on the skin. In particular, many anti-parasite treatments can now be administered by what we call the 'spot-on' method. To apply these, the hair at the back of the neck is parted to reveal the skin. The product is then applied along the line of skin very easily and often without the cat even noticing.

Should I have a first aid kit for my cat?

While being ready in case an accident or emergency happens to your cat is a good idea, there's actually very little you can put in a 'kit'. It's unwise to put any human ointments or potions on cuts or grazes or to use disinfectants, as some such products are toxic to cats. A teaspoonful of salt water in a cup can be used to clean a graze or cut if necessary. If it's a deep cut, then bind it in a cloth or towel and take the cat to the vet.

Likewise, if the cat has been injured in a fall or by a car, has been burned or has collapsed, the veterinary surgery is the best place for it to be. Put it in a carrier or wrap it in a blanket and move it gently into the car, making sure it can't move or slip around during the car journey.

It's very difficult to bandage a cat, and it's likely to simply wriggle out or scratch it off, so veterinary care is invariably the best option.

Regular check ups can help to spot problems early.

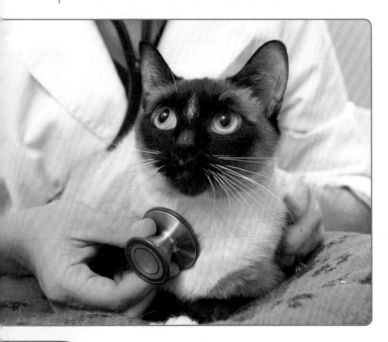

Common problems

Just like people, cats suffer from a wide range of diseases, some caused by infectious agents, others by nutritional problems. Some are more common in older cats and some in younger animals. Some of them are quite complex and there isn't room here to go into all the details, but if you want to know more the Feline Advisory Bureau's website has the most up-to-date and reliable information available on each, including advice on treatment and care.

Infectious diseases

Cats are susceptible to infectious diseases throughout their lives, such as cat flu, enteritis, feline leukaemia and feline immunodeficiency. We can vaccinate against most of these and it's advisable to do so (see page 103).

Feline leukaemia

Feline leukaemia virus (FeLV) affects the immune system by killing or damaging the white blood cells and in this way making the cat susceptible to infection and other disease. Cats which become permanently infected (some will get rid of the virus from their system) are at risk of developing many severe diseases such as anaemia and cancer. Young cats – particularly those less than six months old – are especially vulnerable to becoming permanently infected.

Between 80 and 90 per cent of infected cats die within three and a half years of being diagnosed as having FeLV.

FeLV infection is most common in situations where there's a high population density of cats. This is because a large amount of virus occurs in the saliva of infected cats, and close activities such as grooming and eating from the same food bowls enables it to spread, as may contact with the urine and faeces of infected cats. It can also be passed from a mother cat to her kittens, either in the womb or via infected milk after the kittens are born.

If one of your cats becomes infected you need to consider the health of the others in how you deal with it. Your vet will be able to give you the best advice.

Feline immunodeficiency virus

This virus also affects the cells of the immune system, killing or damaging the white blood cells and thereby affecting the ability of the immune system to fight infection and monitor the body for cancerous cells. Thus FIV-infected cats are at a far greater risk of disease and infection with viruses, bacteria and other organisms.

FIV is usually passed on by biting and fighting, as there are large amounts of virus in the saliva. For this reason unneutered male cats carry a higher risk of infection. A cat can be infected at any age but there can be a long delay between infection and development of clinical signs, and the disease often appears in middle-aged or older cats.

Although FIV is similar to the human form of this virus

(HIV), there is no risk of infection to people in contact with FIV-positive cats.

Cat flu

Cat flu is most commonly seen in situations where cats are kept in large groups such as breeding catteries, rescue centres and feral cat colonies, although it can also occur in pet cat households.

Cat flu is associated with two viruses, feline calicivirus and feline herpesvirus. These affect the respiratory system and the eyes and mouth – infected cats can suffer from sticky sore eyes, ulcers in the mouth and nasal discharge. They may also lose their appetite, have a fever and seem depressed.

In kittens and cats with immune system problems cat flu can be very serious indeed or even fatal. Although most cats do recover some may thereafter suffer from sneezing and 'snotty' periods throughout their lives. Feline herpesvirus stays in the system and if the cat becomes stressed it can suffer from another bout of flu.

This is a very unpleasant disease for cats and owners alike, so it's best to minimise the risk and severity of infection by vaccinating kittens as soon as possible – at eight weeks and then again two weeks later – followed up with annual boosters throughout the rest of their lives, depending on their lifestyle and risk. Both viruses can be carried on clothes, shoes, hands and utensils, so it's easy for cat flu to be passed on even if cats don't actually meet.

Feline enteritis

Although we see this disease less commonly now it's still out there and is extremely unpleasant, causing serious diarrhoea and illness that can be fatal in some cats, especially kittens. The agent is a parvovirus which can survive for a long time in the environment and is hard to kill. It is spread principally via faeces but can also be passed on via food dishes, clothes and hands, as well as on bedding and furniture. Vaccination is very effective and long-lasting.

Feline infectious peritonitis

Feline infectious peritonitis (FIP) is a disease caused by a virus called feline coronavirus. Infection with coronavirus is actually very common but in the majority of cats it doesn't cause a problem. However, occasionally the virus mutates within an infected cat, and it is this changed form that causes the disease known as FIP. It is spread via the litter tray.

Although it can develop at any age, most cases of FIP develop in younger cats, perhaps because their immune systems aren't fully developed. It's thought that the stress of rehoming, neutering, vaccination or other concurrent disease may also make younger cats more likely to succumb.

The disease causes a variety of problems but the characteristic which is most easily recognised is a large fluid-filled abdomen. Infected cats also become lethargic and may not have a large appetite. In some cases the nervous system can be affected and the cat may become wobbly. Unfortunately once the disease is present it usually progresses quite quickly and is invariably fatal.

Ringworm

Ringworm is an infection caused by a fungus that grows on the surface of the skin. The name is rather misleading because it has nothing to do with worms – its actual scientific name is dermatophytosis. It is contagious and is spread by spores found on the hair, which can remain viable for up to two years. Infection can be mild or can cause serious skin disease. A typical skin lesion is roughly circular and the hair falls out, particularly on the head, ears or paws. The skin may look red and inflamed and may be itchy.

Ringworm can also be passed on to people, so an affected cat needs to be treated effectively – your vet is likely to diagnose a drug and perhaps a shampoo to use, and you'll need to try and clean up the house as well. The cat will need to be tested by the vet subsequently to make sure that it's free from the infection.

Nutritional problems

Proper nutrition is vital in cats because they have a much narrower range of foods available to them than, say, dogs or people, both of whom can, if they need to, live on a vegetarian diet.

Most cats are fed on good quality proprietary foods, so it's quite rare now to see cats or kittens suffering from a deficiency of certain nutrients or from underfeeding. Instead, by far the most common nutritional condition, which is causing great concern among those who try to improve pet health, is obesity. Several dog owners have recently been prosecuted under the new Animal Welfare Act for having dogs which are extremely obese.

We have to get our minds around the fact that too much can be as bad as too little. Granted, when an animal is too fat it's probably the result of too much love rather than too little, and an owner who's unable to feed their pet the correct amount because the act of feeding is associated in their mind with caring; whereas an animal which demonstrates an equivalent deficiency of body weight is probably the result of neglect, either in feeding or the failure to treat an illness. But the results can be the same for the animal. In our newspapers we regularly see pictures

---

Prevention is always better than cure

For all of the reasons outlined above, if a problem in a cat can be avoided then it's worth doing so! Therefore preventive care such as vaccinations, regular flea and worm treatment and check-ups are well worthwhile. As an owner it's also very useful to make yourself familiar with your cat's normal weight, its food likes and dislikes and its behaviour patterns, so that when small changes start to occur you'll notice. There are pointers to help you with this on page 94.

of cats which are almost square because they're carrying so much weight, and references to 'fat cats' are often made in jest, but it's not funny and the excess weight will cause these cats many problems and increase their susceptibility to disorders such as diabetes and arthritis.

See page 106 for more information on feeding.

Dental disease

If your cat is over three years old it's quite likely it will have some tooth and gum disease. Cats often suffer from something called 'neck' lesions, which are areas – often under the gum (hence the name) – where teeth seem to have been absorbed, leaving holes which can be very painful. Such teeth will probably need to be extracted. So it's important to have your cat's mouth checked regularly, ideally during its annual check-up.

It's also worth bearing in mind that many insurance policies don't cover dental treatment except for fractures, and others will only cover it if your cat has been given regular dental examinations and care, if advised by your vet.

Dental disease can lead to bad breath and loss of appetite because of discomfort when eating, and infections in the mouth can also affect other organs.

Kidney problems

The kidneys are amazing organs – they can become diseased or get damaged but can still keep the cat functioning normally for a long time. Hence by the time we see signs of kidney disease in our cats – drinking more and urinating more because the kidneys have lost much of their ability to concentrate urine – only about a quarter of the kidneys may be working.

The kidneys are vital to life and health in that they're involved with water balance in the body and with getting rid of waste. If they're not working well the cat is likely to feel unwell and will probably lose its appetite. This, of course, means the body doesn't receive the nutrition it needs, which can compound problems.

There are medical and dietary treatments that can help to maintain the part of the kidney which is still functioning, and owners can even help to rehydrate their cats using subcutaneous fluids if they and their vet feel they're happy to do this and it's appropriate for that cat. Once more, the earlier this problem can be picked up the sooner the kidneys can be cared for.

Kidney problems mostly affect older cats and it's recommended that cats over seven years old have urine tests and those over eleven years old have a blood test to check for problems. Cats over fifteen years old should visit the vet twice a year, as kidney and other problems are far more likely to be present.

Diabetes

Diabetes mellitus is most commonly encountered in cats aged between about seven and ten years, and as in humans is caused by a lack of insulin. Insulin is produced by

Feline couch potato!

the pancreas and released into the bloodstream, where it travels to all the tissues of the body. Its main role is to enable cells to take up glucose (sugar), which is needed as an energy source. If glucose isn't available to the cells they start to use fat and protein for energy and this can result in loss of weight and other problems. Glucose is lost in urine, and as urine volume increases so the cat drinks more. This results in the signs most commonly associated with diabetes (but which are also signs of other diseases, including hyperthyroidism and kidney disease) – weight loss despite a large appetite, and increased drinking.

The earlier that diabetes can be detected the better, so routine urine checks in cats above seven years old are recommended. Diabetes is usually a treatable condition, and although it requires considerable dedication and commitment from owners it can be a very rewarding problem to manage.

There are several things to consider – if the cat is obese this may well have caused or contributed to the diabetes, and tackling its obesity may help considerably in the treatment of the diabetes. There are also prescription low carbohydrate pet foods for diabetic cats. However, most diabetic cats will require insulin injections, at least initially, and your vet will be able to show you how to do this. In some cases the diabetes will resolve itself, in others the cat will need treatment for life.

Hyperthyroidism

One of the diseases which has come to light in cats in the past 15 years is a condition called feline hyperthyroidism. This is caused by over-activity of the thyroid gland, which affects, among other things, the metabolic activities of the body. Cats suffering from hyperthyroidism are often very hungry and eat a lot but lose weight, and their coats look in poor condition.

There are medical treatments for hyperthyroidism. The gland can be removed surgically or, if you're lucky enough to be near a veterinary school or a practice with the facilities, you can treat it with radioactive iodine, which is very effective. Hyperthyroid cats may have heart problems and blood pressure problems too, so your vet will also check for these.

Arthritis

It's only recently that we've come to understand quite how common arthritis is in older cats. Because the cat is so brilliant at hiding discomfort and pain and doesn't limp dramatically in the way a dog can, we assume that it's fine; but when researchers actually looked at X-ray pictures of older cats' joints they found lots of damage. When they treated affected cats with anti-inflammatory medication owners reported that their cats had become like kittens again, jumping up just like they used to and moving around much more.

The trouble is that the disorder comes on slowly and we don't always notice the behavioural changes, especially if the cat is doing less rather than doing something different or bizarre. But cats affected by arthritis are less likely to jump up to high places where perhaps they used to rest, or to jump down or climb the stairs, and they may become much less active simply because doing things hurts. But

they're unlikely to limp, cry out or do anything dramatic, so it's up to owners to become detectives and, as explained earlier, to take notice of behavioural changes and seek help for their cats if they feel they may be in discomfort.

Can you catch diseases from your cat or can your cat catch diseases from you?

There are a few diseases and parasites which we can share with our cats. Animal diseases that are transmissible to humans are called zoonotic diseases, but for most people they're rare and of little danger. However, some people are at much greater risk, often because their immune system isn't working properly. High risk groups include babies, the elderly, ill people and people who are what we term immunosuppressed – for example, someone having anticancer therapy, those with AIDS or people on medication to prevent organ rejection after a transplant. For these people any infection, be it from an animal or another person, can be serious. Nevertheless, it remains much more common for people to acquire infections from other people than from pets. Occasionally people can even give diseases to cats – an example would be MRSA.

Many of the diseases cats get are species-specific, *ie* they only occur in cats – examples of these would be feline leukaemia, feline immunodeficiency virus and cat flu – but some, such as ringworm, toxocara, toxoplasmosis and a few gastrointestinal problems, are transmissible. Pregnant women should be especially careful but shouldn't panic. There's no need to get rid of the cat; just use gloves to clean out the litter tray or use it as an excuse to get someone else to do it! However, the risk is low and can be minimised by adhering to good common-sense hygiene.

If you have someone from one of the higher risk categories in your home then it's very important to think about the following:

- Wash your hands after handling animals or animal waste, as well as before eating, cleaning your teeth, handling contact lenses or smoking.
- Keep litter trays clean and away from food preparation areas.
- Remove uneaten food so that it doesn't go off.
- Keep human utensils and dishes separate from the cat's.
- If the cat has diarrhoea anyone at higher risk should avoid cleaning up the litter tray or should wear gloves and do it in a well-ventilated environment. Disinfect the tray and all surrounding areas.

If you're bitten or scratched by your cat you should always wash the site immediately. If you have a wound that your cat licks this should also be washed. If you get bitten go to your doctor – cat bites tend to be puncture wounds, which can close up almost immediately leaving a pocket of infection behind that can become serious. High risk individuals especially should be very careful.

Keep your cat vaccinated and treated for fleas and worms, keep its litter tray clean and disinfected and wash your hands regularly. This is all common sense and part of good cat care anyway.

If you need more information on any of the diseases mentioned here visit the websites of the Feline Advisory Bureau or the Cat Group (see page 140 for contact details).

Your cat's life

How long do cats live?

For their size, cats live quite a long time. Generally an animal's longevity is proportional to its size (with the exception of tortoises, man and a few other animals). A tiny mouse has a short lifespan, a rabbit somewhat longer and a dog between 7 and 20 years depending on its breed or size, its activity, or both. Cats aren't much bigger than rabbits, but whereas the rabbit may live about 8 years a cat will live on average about 12–14 years, and it's not unusual for cats to reach their late teens or even their early 20s.

Some say this disproportional longevity is because cats sleep a lot. They do seem to be quite healthy animals, perhaps because they're still mostly what we call moggies or mixtures – *ie* the selection process is still mostly the random result of an encounter between a tom and an unneutered queen, and therefore still in effect the survival of the fittest (or at least, those whose reproductive organs have escaped the vet's scalpel!). The problem with pedigree animals is that they're bred from a limited number of animals with a small gene pool, and are often all related in

some way. If a problem arises in such a small group it can then become what's called an inherited disorder, which spreads throughout the tightly related group because there's little fresh input of genes. Having said that, however, some pedigree breeds such as Siamese and Burmese do actually seem to frequently live into their late teens, so any problems that may exist within a breed won't necessarily be life-threatening or life-shortening.

In my day job at the Feline Advisory Bureau, the health of cats, and how owners and vets can help cats to live long and healthy lives, is something we examine constantly. During its 50th anniversary in 2008 FAB launched a huge project called WellCat for Life, where we took a fresh look at cats and how we regard their ages and stages of life. What we wanted to do was make the way we think about our cats' age and health much more relevant. To do this we considered the stages a cat's life goes through. We came up with six life-stages – the six ages of cat, you might say (see illustration).

Working with the FAB feline expert panel, consisting of vets who've specialised in cat treatment and care, the stages were calculated to take into

	Life stage	Age of cat	Human equivalent
Tigger **3 months old**	**Kitten** birth to 6 months	0 – 1 month 2 – 3 months 4 months 6 months	0 – 1 year 2 – 4 years 6 – 8 years 10 years
Sugar **13 months old**	**Junior** 7 months to 2 years	7 months 12 months 18 months 2 years	12 years 15 years 21 years 24 years
Rosie **3 years old**	**Prime** 3 years to 6 years	3 4 5 6	28 32 36 40
Nemo **8 years old**	**Mature** 7 years to 10 years	7 8 9 10	44 48 52 56
George **13 years old**	**Senior** 11 years to 14 years	11 12 13 14	60 64 68 72
Chinarose **16 years old**	**Geriatric** 15 years+	15 16 17 18 19 20 21 22 23 24 25	76 80 84 88 92 96 100 104 108 112 116

Courtesy of the Feline Advisory Bureau.

account, growth, behaviour and the times when cats are more likely to suffer from different problems. For example, stage one is 'Kitten', and covers the first six months of a cat's life – a period when the young cat is growing rapidly and is usually not quite sexually mature. 'Junior' runs from kitten to about two years old; during this time the cat reaches full size and learns about life and how to survive it. The period from three to six years old is called 'Prime', when the cat is mature physically and behaviourally, and is still usually healthy and active, looking sleek and shiny and making the best of life. From seven to ten the cat is what we call 'Mature', equivalent to humans in their mid-40s to mid-50s. The 'Senior' stage ranges from 11 to 14 years and takes the cat up to the equivalent of about 70 human years. Finally, the word 'geriatric' is used for cats over 15 years old – and many cats do reach this stage, some not showing any signs of being geriatric at all!

The table opposite shows all of the stages and also the equivalent human age. What these stages let us do is to appreciate how old the cat is inside, since, as has been pointed out, this is often not very obvious from the outside, as cats seldom go grey or show outward signs of pain or illnesses such as arthritis.

Prevention of disease

Vaccination

Fifty years ago we couldn't even identify most of the diseases that affected cats. Many cats died from diseases that we probably recognised as infectious – *ie* that cats caught off one another – but we couldn't identify the infectious organisms or even try to control them. But we've come a long way in 50 years. If you talk to people who were involved in cat rescue back then they'll tell you that tackling cat flu and feline enteritis was a daily consequence of our inability to protect our cats. These days, however, we have vaccines against most of the infectious diseases that affect cats and we should make use of them. Yes, we worry about the side-effects of vaccinations, and although these are generally mild – such as a small lump at the site which disappears after a couple of weeks, or the cat being slightly quiet or seemingly off-colour for a day – a cat might very occasionally react more seriously; very, very occasionally a lump appears at the injection site which does *not* disappear – if this happens, check with your vet. However, the risks are small and vaccinations help to protect most cats against diseases which can be life-threatening or, at the very least, can cause diseases that are unpleasant and potentially long-lasting. Vaccinations aren't 100 per cent effective, but they do provide good protection, and if a vaccinated cat does still pick up the virus the disease it causes is usually a much less severe.

Vaccines are available for a number of different diseases, mostly those caused by viruses. The viruses we worry about are feline herpesvirus and calicivirus, both components of cat flu, and panelukopenia virus, which causes feline enteritis or serious diarrhoea and other symptoms that, in young kittens, can be fatal. These are the basic diseases against which we need to vaccinate. The viruses are not only passed from cat to cat but can also be carried on our own hands, clothes and shoes, so that even if your cat doesn't meet other cats or go outside, it's still worth protecting against them. If your cat does go outdoors you should also consider protecting it against feline leukaemia virus. Unfortunately we don't yet have a vaccine against feline immunodeficiency virus in the UK.

A booster to maintain immunity is recommended at about one year old, and thereafter it's worth talking to your vet about when to give boosters in the future. This can depend very much on the lifestyle of your cat. If you have a huntin', shootin', fishin' sort of cat which is out and about meeting and even fighting with other cats, he will probably need protection against everything possible on a regular basis! If, on the other hand, you have a cat that stays indoors and doesn't meet other cats, then you may only need to provide protection against the diseases that can be transmitted on shoes or clothes, but not those that require cat-to-cat contact. If your cat regularly goes into a cattery or is a show cat, then again you're putting it into potentially higher-risk scenarios and annual vaccination will be necessary; indeed, sight of an up-to-date inoculation record will usually be required by show organisers and cattery owners alike.

Some research has suggested that vaccines may actually last longer than the one year that manufacturers have to guarantee them for, but again it's a matter of balancing risk. This is something to talk over with your vet. What's important is to give your cat as much protection as you can.

Flea treatment

We're lucky that we're past the time when the only approach to flea treatment in cats was to spray them with chemicals such as organophosphates. This treatment was not without its problems on several levels. Such chemicals are now recognised as being dangerous, and the method by which they were applied to the cat was probably its least favourite activity! As has been explained, cats hiss as a sign of displeasure, fear and defiance, so they're usually keen to avoid a spraying, hissing can at any cost. Having to be held down and sprayed with something that smells very strong and unpleasant is no doubt very stressful for a cat too.

The only alternatives to using a spray used to be powders or combing using a flea comb, but in the past decade or so we've come a long way from that. We now have some very effective chemicals available that affect fleas (but not cats), and a method of application that the cat doesn't mind and often doesn't even notice. These new chemicals kill fleas or interrupt their lifecycle by interfering with physiological pathways specific to insects, and so are much safer. They're applied by parting the fur and putting a small amount of the compound on to the skin at the back of the cat's neck. From here it's distributed over the whole body. Such chemicals work for about a month on average, thus protection is very effective. The cat hardly notices that anything has happened, especially if you apply it gently and smoothly while you're grooming or even giving a little treat. The most effective treatments are available through your vet, although some are also now available through country stores and large pet shops.

Always ask for advice if you're not sure which one to use, because there's one thing you need to be very, *very* careful about if you treat your cat with one of these products. Such back-of-the-neck treatments are all lumped together and referred to as 'spot-ons', which is a reference to the mode of application rather than the different chemicals involved. But you need to be aware that there are also dog products called spot-ons, which contain a concentrated chemical called permethrin which, if applied to cats, can be fatal. Although permethrin is an effective insecticide and doesn't harm dogs, cats can't tolerate it, and it can cause convulsions and even death.

Every year many cats suffer poisoning from permethrin. The sad thing is that these poisonings are accidental and totally preventable – owners don't realise that they shouldn't use the dog product on their cat, or think that they can just use a little bit because 'a cat is like a small dog', or they lost the packaging and missed the warning on it, or they simply use it by accident. Most owners feel absolutely terrible when it happens, and the cat usually needs intensive treatment in the veterinary surgery, often for a couple of days, in order to stand any chance of recovery. Some of the cats don't recover, or owners feel they can't afford the treatment, so the outcome can be very sad. The take-home message is *never* use a dog flea-product on a cat, and if you have both dogs and cats, and have lots of flea-treatment pipettes all muddled up in the pet medicine drawer, *always* double-check that you're using the right one.

Also be aware that cats can sometimes be affected by curling up with a dog that's just been treated for fleas, or can become poisoned if they groom the dog. So if you treat your dog with a spot-on treatment containing permethrin (these are usually the ones purchased from supermarkets or petshops), keep it away from the cat for a day or two so that the cat isn't affected. Don't comb the cat if you've just combed the dog after treating it either.

Don't take a risk. *Always* check that the flea products you put on your cat are *designed* for cats.

Other skin parasites

Occasionally cats get ticks, which are insects that live in the grass and hitch a ride on passing animals, climbing through their hair and burrowing their heads into the skin to feed on blood. They start off small and swell to the size of a small pea as they fill up, before they drop off. They can cause disease, so it's worth removing them when you find them. However, it's not just a case of pulling them off – if you try to do this you often remove the body but leave the head in the skin, and it can become infected, so it's best to get a special tick remover (available from your vet or a pet shop). You can also use the liquid form of a product called Frontline, which is available in a pump spray. Spraying a little onto the tick will kill it.

Some of the good flea products also treat lice and mites, but if your cat is becoming itchy it's worth checking with your vet regarding what skin parasite or condition you're dealing with, and then take their advice on the most appropriate treatment.

Worming

Cats can get two sorts of worms – round worms and tape worms. Roundworms are very common. If your cat has them you may see some in its litter tray (greyish white, long and thin), but often you won't even know your cat has them. Eggs can be passed from cat to cat in faeces or by eating prey. Kittens also get roundworms via their mother's milk and should be treated from about six weeks old.

Tapeworms are long, flat and made up of lots of segments. The cat will pick up their eggs from eating prey or by ingesting an infected flea which in turn ingested an egg when it was in its larval form. You may notice small segments looking like rice grains under the cat's tail. Cats which go outdoors and hunt will need regular treatment every two to three months, but indoor cats may go for longer than this. Again, check with your vet regarding your own particular cat and its lifestyle. Fleas can transmit tapeworms by passing on their eggs, so flea treatment is essential too.

Worm treatments can be given in the form of tablets or granules, and are also now available in 'spot-on' form – *ie* in liquid form that can be administered by parting the hair and putting it on to the skin at the back of the neck in the same way as flea preparations. This makes worming your cat much easier and removes the need to fight over tablet giving, although many tablets are also more palatable to cats today.

Neutering your kitten

In the UK cat owners are pretty good about getting their cats neutered – over 90 per cent ensure that this is done, so that helping to prevent an excess of unwanted kittens. Of course, there are still plenty of cats that need new homes,

still kittens being born, usually because their owners haven't realised in time that their own 'kitten' is now grown up and the tom from around the corner has noticed before they have!

Neutering female cats reduces the risk of mammary cancer and uterine infection as well as, obviously, preventing them from coming into season and exhibiting the signs of being on 'heat' that can be somewhat difficult to live with. Female cats 'call', or miaow loudly, and constantly try to encourage all the boys in town to come around. If the cat isn't neutered and doesn't become pregnant this behaviour can continue every few weeks from January through to October. And although moggies are pretty slick at giving birth and looking after their kittens, there are risks involved in pregnancy and lactation. Caring for the kittens may also not be plain sailing, as they can suffer from illnesses and are susceptible to infectious diseases, although the main problem may be finding good homes for them where you can be sure they'll be loved and cared for.

Neutered males will stay closer to home, as they don't need to range far afield to find female cats in season to mate with. They won't be so aggressive or competitive either, and so are less likely to get into fights – fight injuries can be serious, with abscesses being common, and fighting is a very good way to pass on diseases such as feline immunodeficiency disease (FIV), the feline equivalent of HIV. An unneutered tom is also likely to spray pungent urine indoors, and certainly around the garden or the neighbour's garden, which many not be appreciated!

Traditionally kittens have been neutered at six months old. However, these days a slightly earlier age of four months is recommended. This is because at six months old some kittens are sufficiently mature to become pregnant (owners often only begin to think about neutering at six months and the cat's probably nearer seven or eight months old by the time they get around to it, by which time the females are often already pregnant). Also veterinary care, knowledge and anaesthesia techniques have improved greatly and the care available for smaller, younger animals is now excellent.

The benefits of earlier neutering are that younger kittens bounce back and recover from the operation very quickly indeed. If you get a kitten from a rescue centre it's likely to be neutered already – indeed, it may have been neutered as early as two to three months old without any harm. Likewise breeders too are now selling kittens that have already been neutered. People who work with feral cats will neuter kittens when they can catch them – they may not get another chance, so these may be neutered very early. All the scientific evidence shows that are no problems associated with early neutering, and there are actually many benefits.

Feeding – it's about more than just the food

The most important thing to remember is that your cat is an obligate carnivore – meaning its natural diet must include meat in order to provide it with a high enough level of protein and all of the nutrients essential to its health and wellbeing. Think about a cat in the wild; it eats very little vegetable matter – it may nibble at grass or a few herbs and may take in some vegetable material from the gut of animals that it eats, but this constitutes only a very small part of its diet. And because it's such a successful hunter the cat hasn't had to resort to scavenging, so that its body has dispensed with (or never had) some of the biological pathways which exist in other animals – such as the dog – that enable them to deal

experience. Besides, it's a great insult to expect an animal that's evolved to become an almost perfect predator to eat food that isn't natural to it.

How do you choose a food for your cat? The first thing to consider is its age – a kitten will need a diet that's designed to give it the energy and nutrients needed for rapid growth, while the more mature cat (just like mature people) may not need so much. Obesity is in fact becoming a problem in cats because of readily accessible food and perhaps a lack of exercise. In addition most of us don't read the pack to see how much food is recommended for the cat and probably overfeed them. Neutering reduces a cat's energy expenditure, and neutered cats can be a lot less active and so more likely to put on weight. Neutering may also increase appetite, so owners may have to control their cat's food intake a bit to stop them becoming fat.

While cats can be very good at regulating their own food intake, they're tempted by very palatable foods. In addition if they don't venture outdoors so much they may eat as a result of being bored. It may also be that the way we feed them obliges them to eat in a way that overrides their natural ability to limit their own intake. Experts now say that if kittens are fed on an intermittent basis from an early age, and the food is hidden or has to be worked for in a 'puzzle feeder' – a dispenser which releases pieces of food as the cat plays with or explores it, such as a plastic ball with holes in it which allow the food to escape as the cat bats the ball (there are several sorts on the market, or you can make your own) – they're more likely to regulate their own intake. If we just plonk some very attractive or palatable food in a dish twice a day and it's only available or fresh for a short period of time, the cat may keep eating past the sensation of fullness and will lose its ability to regulate its own intake to a healthy level. The trouble is, if you then change to an intermittent dry-food diet the cat

with less 'pure' input. The cat's liver doesn't contain the same chemical pathways and enzymes as a dog's and consequently can't synthesise some of its essential requirements from other materials – it therefore needs to ingest them directly from other animals that have done the work for them. For this reason dog food isn't suitable for cats, as it lacks these feline-essential nutrients. (As we will see in the section on poisoning, some of the detoxifying pathways present in dogs and other creatures also don't exist in cats, making them susceptible to poisons used on other animals.)

Not only is trying to feed a cat a vegetarian diet very dangerous to its health, but it also won't enjoy the

Wet or dry?

There are many good-quality commercial diets available for cats, some 'wet' – either in cans, foil trays or pouches – and some 'dry'. The advantage of dry food is that it can be supplied intermittently for the cat to nibble throughout the day, as and when it feels the need, which is more like a cat's natural feeding rhythm than just having one or two large meals. Wet food, on the other hand, goes off quite quickly, especially in warm weather, and needs to be removed and replaced with fresh frequently.

Cats usually eat their food fresh and warm, and may not be so well equipped as a dog to deal with food that's spoiled and may consequently contain toxins. Dogs are used to scavenging and eating food that's well past its 'sell-by' date (those of us who have owned Labradors, for instance, will have seen them eat the most hideous mouldy or maggot-ridden food that they've found during

a walk, without showing the slightest stomach problems or any other reaction later on). But the more fastidious cat doesn't like old food and will be quite picky about what it eats.

may overeat this as well, so you may need to help by restricting the amount available over the whole day, but not when the cat can eat it.

Cats also have us very well trained. They know that by miaowing or by rubbing against us they can initiate a response. And people automatically feed them, to please them – we just assume that this type of interaction is a request for food, and feeding them is an easy option. In fact it may simply be a request for interaction with us, but as owners we want to give them something more, and so the cat gets more food.

You may not have ever thought about where you feed your cat or how you feed several cats that live together. In the wild cats will eat alone, so putting lots of dishes in a line for a group of cats and feeding all of them at the same time may be very stressful for some of them. They may act as if they aren't bothered, but if there's competition for food in one area at one time they may have to overcome these emotions to get to it.

As we learn more about the behaviour and preferences of cats we've come to realise that feeding them as we would feed ourselves – ie with a couple of meals a day provided on a plate – isn't really 'thinking cat', and is making quite a few anthropomorphic assumptions.

Think instead about how a cat feeds in the wild, where you could perhaps describe it as a snacker and snoozer, taking in small amounts of food on a regular basis. It explores an area and identifies prey or places to watch for prey. It hunts many times a day and probably eats about ten rodents or birds, after several attempts at trying to catch each meal. And during all of this the cat will usually eat alone, unless it has kittens. This cycle of hunting and eating goes on throughout the day and night, and in the process the cat regulates its own intake so that it stays at a healthy weight. Ideally, therefore, this is the kind of eating pattern that we should try to replicate in a domestic environment.

Some cats seem to change their minds every day regarding what they like to eat, and keep their owners running backwards and forwards to the supermarket to find a new flavour or brand, which they then go off in turn after a week or two. Whether this is because some cats like

variety or just like to keep us guessing and under control is hard to say! Some cats may well have another home, or even two, which they visit during the day and where they may be given treats or even food which they like better, making them less hungry when they return home.

Some cats go the other way, and will only eat one type of food. If this is a complete diet which gives them all of their nutritional requirements, then that shouldn't be a problem. If, however, it's something like tuna or chicken breasts then it won't be giving the cat everything it needs and you'll need to try and introduce new, more nutritional foods gradually, mixed in with the cat's preferred food.

We also often misinterpret our cat's behaviour with us and offer food in return for, for example, the cat rubbing around our legs or jumping up onto the table or chair to interact with us. In this way we may provide too much food rather than just giving them the attention they seek.

What a cat likes or dislikes eating is partly controlled by genetics and partly by experience. Cats are said to like variety in what they eat and may often choose something new rather than something they're used to. However, if they're feeling under stress cats will tend to choose a food that they're familiar with, which will give them a feeling of security – something that's recognisable when other things in their life are not under control. Thus if your cat is going into a cattery while you're on holiday make sure that the cattery feeds it its regular food to help it settle in.

Even *where* you feed your cat can have an effect on how much or when it eats – it may be noisy or very bright, it may be associated with a bad event, or the type of food may be associated with an illness.

It doesn't really matter what the food dish itself is made of. As for the shape, cats probably prefer wide shallow dishes which don't move around as they eat. What's more important is that you ensure that it's kept clean and that any wet food is removed frequently so that it doesn't begin to go rancid. As mentioned elsewhere, cats like their food and water to be separated so it's probably best to avoid using a double-bowl, putting food on one side and water on the other – not least because the food often contaminates the water if they're that close.

Don't forget water

You also need to think about water. Cats in the wild eat small animals that have a very high water content. Although cats were originally desert animals and are able to maintain good control of their water intake and loss, they do need water. They can survive if water availability is low from time to time because they can concentrate their urine and so lose as little water as possible. However, not taking in enough water on a regular basis – and remember, if you feed it dry food your cat will need a great deal more water than if it ate wet food (which is over 80 per cent water) – may predispose the cat to problems such as cystitis. Also, kidney disease is common in older cats and it's very important with this disease that they keep up their water intake.

In the wild water and food would seldom be found together and food would not be located next to water. Yet in our homes, who among us hasn't put the water dish next to the food dish for the convenience of the cat (and probably ourselves)? Putting the water in a separate and, if you have a number of cats, a number of different areas may encourage cats to drink.

In the wild water may well be flowing and therefore fresh. Once again, cats don't do the dog thing of drinking from stagnant puddles, and may prefer running water if they can get it. This is perhaps because a cat's body is less able to deal with the contaminants and toxins that occur in stagnant water, and they therefore avoid it. Saying that, cats do have drinking foibles. Some prefer rainwater, some pond water, some water from the toilet, and others water from a dripping tap. Many cats seem to enjoy drinking from fountains where the water is running continuously. Some people also suggest that certain types of material, such as plastic, give water a flavour that cats don't enjoy, and recommend using glass, ceramic or metal water dishes.

Cats generally don't like their whiskers being touched, since they're extremely sensitive instruments and are capable of very flexible movements that enable the cat to use them in avoiding obstacles. Consequently if the cat has to push its whiskers against the sides of a bowl in order to lap up water, because the container is narrow, deep and not kept full, this can limit the time it's prepared to drink for. Using a flat wide dish and keeping the water fresh and topped up may help.

If you feed your cat dry food, make sure there's plenty of fresh water around. If your cat suffers from kidney or bladder problems it's best to avoid dry food anyway and opt for a wetter diet that ensures it ingests more water.

Though we often associate cats with milk, and some much prefer it to water when they can get it, it doesn't agree with all of them. This is because when cats are kittens they have an enzyme which helps them to digest milk, but as they get older they stop producing this enzyme because an adult cat in the wild would seldom have access to milk. Thus it can be difficult for adult cats to digest milk and it may cause stomach upset. However, the wonders of modern pet-keeping mean that we can now buy milk made especially for our feline friends which doesn't upset them.

Special diets

There are also special diets that can be prescribed by a vet to help tackle kidney problems, arthritis and other disorders such as liver and digestive problems, or to aid recovery from illness or an operation. These can be a very useful way to help a cat, but require a veterinary diagnosis first because they'll contain more or less of certain ingredients in order to tackle a specific medical condition, and so may not be suitable for every cat.

If a special diet is required in the management of a disease condition, it's best to introduce it gradually while the cat still has access to its original diet (unless the vet suggests otherwise). This lets the cat become familiar with the new diet and learn that it's safe to eat it. Sadly, cats sometimes don't like a special diet because it's not very palatable – it doesn't have those things which tick feline boxes – much as we might think something is in need of more salt or is a texture or flavour that we don't enjoy. There are several pet food manufacturers who produce special diets for different conditions, so there may be several to choose from if your cat is not fond of a particular one. However, you'll need to take your vet's advice as to what to do, since not eating the diet properly may affect your cat's condition.

The right weight for your cat

Obesity isn't only a problem for people and dogs, it's creeping into the feline population too. In a nutshell, fat cats seem to be becoming more common.

Most of us neuter our cats because it's the responsible thing to do. It makes our pet cats much easier to live with, it has health benefits (or helps to avoid health risks), and it prevents the birth of kittens that may not all find good homes. But neutering also reduces activity. Let's face it, if you're not driven by hormones to wander the countryside fighting off other males then you're more likely to stay in the warm and avoid conflict if you can. You'll be more laid-back and other things will become more interesting – such as food.

Scientists have established that male cats experience an increase in appetite that can result in them eating 25 per cent more food than an unneutered cat. Apparently neutered cats also use 30 per cent less energy than entire cats, as the cat's metabolic rate, which could be defined as the sort of rev rate it normally lives at, slows after neutering. So if a neutered cat eats the same amount of food as an unneutered it will be laid down as fat. And if it eats more it will be laid down as yet more fat.

All of this points to the need for owners to take responsibility for not letting their cats get too fat, because cats will suffer the same sorts of problems as people and dogs do from being overweight (ie arthritis, heart disease and diabetes among other things). There's also something very wrong in seeing this normally lithe and active creature sitting there too fat to bother to get up and too wide to use the cat flap!

However, as usual, cats don't put on weight in quite the same way as dogs. Some can carry quite a lot of weight slung underneath their tummy, like a sort of apron of fat. Certain breeds, such as the Burmese, are very good at this, but moggies too can carry their extra weight in this way. So how can you tell if your cat is overweight?

First of all it's very useful if you can get a sort of base reference weight for your cat when it's *not* fat. This obviously requires a bit of thinking ahead. If you can note your cat's weight when it's fully grown (ie when it's about two years old), while it's still active and hasn't yet turned into a couch potato, then you'll know what you're aiming to maintain. It's very easy to overfeed cats so you'll need to take control if yours is getting fat. But talk to your vet first, because it's dangerous for cats to lose weight too quickly, or to not eat for a couple of days. A slow and steady approach is required.

Veterinary surgeries often use similar scales to those used to weigh newborn babies – they have a big 'tray' in which the cat can sit or stand and feel secure while the reading is taken. Getting a cat to actually sit or stand for long enough

on bathroom scales at home can be pretty frustrating. It's best to weigh yourself and then pick up the cat and weigh both of you, the difference being the cat's weight.

You'll also need to know what your cat's weight *should* be. Cats usually weigh between about 3kg and 6kg (6½–13lb). In addition you need to do what's called a 'body condition score' for your own cat. If its ribs are very visible and you can't feel any fat on its body then it may actually be too thin, and you'll need to have it checked over by your vet – it may have an illness that's affecting it. When a cat's at its ideal weight the ribs can be felt but the sensation is softened by tissue between the skin and bone. It won't have any obvious bulges when you look at it from above and there'll be no fat swinging under its tummy. As it puts on weight the ribs become harder to feel and there may be slight sagging under the tummy; the cat will look more solid, and at this stage you can label it 'overweight'. The term 'obese' applies when the cat's ribs are difficult to feel through the thick layer of fat beneath its skin and it has a really baggy pad of fat hanging under its abdomen.

If you use both techniques – weighing and assessing – once or twice a year you'll get a good idea of your cat's weight and be able to avoid it accumulating excess fat. At the same time, obviously, if your cat shows signs of losing weight you need to seek veterinary advice. It may have a dental problem or it may be unwell.

Tips for getting an ill cat to eat

Having looked at preventing obesity in cats that are eating too much, it's important to be aware that cats can also go the other way and suffer from a lack of appetite if they're

upset or unwell. If that happens you'll need to try and coax them to eat, which can sometimes be difficult. Cats do, however, respond well to tender loving care, since understandably they get depressed when they're unwell and that can be why they don't want to eat.

If your cat has had an operation or has

a serious illness it may not feel like eating when you take it home. The trouble with not eating is that it's a vicious circle for the cat – it feels unwell and doesn't want to eat, without food it feels weak and more unwell, and so on. If it doesn't eat its body will start to break down body tissue for energy in order to function, and this can slow healing, so eating is very important to recovery. Otherwise the immune system may not function properly, making the cat more susceptible to infection, and the way the cat's body responds to the drugs intended to make it better may even be affected.

Unlike dogs, which can go without food for some time without serious consequences, cats can develop a problem called hepatic lipidosis, a disease of the liver which can be fatal. This can develop if a cat doesn't eat even for a relatively short time (two to three days). We also know that cats have very specific needs when it comes to nutrients, and a lack of these can be dangerous too. The problem is that cats are usually not so food-orientated as dogs and can be finicky eaters, so it can be difficult to encourage them to start eating sometimes.

Are there certain foods that you just can't face because something about them makes you feel ill? Well, cats are the same. They may avoid a certain food because they associate it with feelings of nausea that they had with a particular illness. This is called food aversion and can contribute to a cat's loss of appetite. Food aversion can occur when a cat is feeling ill and is continuously offered a particular food or is even force-fed. The cat associates the feeling of illness with that food and will therefore try to avoid it. So if your cat seems to be lacking in appetite, don't leave the food down, and never try to force-feed it using a syringe.

When a cat loses its appetite you want to try all sorts of things to get it eating again. Owners often turn to baby food because it's soft and easy to lap, and perhaps they feel it's nourishing and reassuring too. The trouble is that many baby foods include powdered onion or garlic to help flavour the food, but onion is toxic to cats so food containing it won't help your cat to recover!

So what can you do to encourage your cat to eat?

First of all you can ensure the cat is comfortable and feeling secure (see Chapter 6). Give it some space away from other cats and dogs that might be making it feel it has to compete for attention, good sleeping spots and even food. As I've said, cats respond to tender loving care, and spending a little time sitting with your cat, giving it some attention and putting small pieces of food on your finger to be licked off might just help to get it started. Illness can result in food just not tasting of very much, but eating even a little may help to release the aromas and make food more appealing again. So will using strong-flavoured foods such as fish, or tasty food such as chicken or prawns.

If your cat has to avoid too much salt or some other ingredient as part of its treatment, it's worth checking with your vet whether particular foods are off the menu. The vet may even prescribe a food that's specially developed to aid recovery. Offer the cat little bits, praising it frequently, and stay close by if that's what reassures it and helps it to relax and eat. If the cat doesn't eat, then remove the food and try again a little later.

Regular health monitoring

If you regularly vaccinate, worm and de-flea your cat then you're ensuring that preventable diseases and parasites won't compromise its health. But of course, there are lots of other health matters to consider, the most important of which is good old 'watching'. Knowing what's normal behaviour for your cat and taking notice if something seems unusual is key to picking up problems. Follow your instincts. Cat owners usually know their cats very well, so if you have suspicions of any of the following then watch even more closely and take advice or visit your vet just to check:

- Is your cat quieter, sleeping more, grooming less or withdrawing from handling? Is it behaving is a way which you don't expect?
- Is your cat drinking more or less than normal?
- Is your cat's poo any different? Does the cat have difficulty in passing motions or is it constipated (common in older cats)?
- Is your cat weeing more or less, is it doing it in strange places, or is it experiencing difficulty?
- Is your cat eating as normal? Does it seem to have difficulty picking up the food or chewing? Does it seem to be hungry but then not interested in eating?
- Is your cat's coat sleek and well groomed or is it matted or 'staring' (hairs standing up with an unkempt, almost greasy look)?
- Are your cat's eyes and ears clean and clear? Is it sneezing or coughing?
- Has your cat's body posture changed? Does it seem a little hunched?

As cats get older they may also suffer from stiffness and arthritis. The trouble is that these changes happen slowly and unless we take a fresh look at the cat we may not notice. So take a look at the list of questions below, which might help you decide whether your cat is having mobility problems:

- Does your cat seem less willing to jump up and down? Does it not sleep on its favourite windowsill any more, or jump up on the table or cupboard?
- Does your cat stay downstairs much more than it used to?
- Is your cat asking you to open the door rather than using the cat flap?
- Will your cat not jump on your lap from the floor any more, but instead climb up slowly via various stools and cushions to make his way over to you?
- Does your cat seem less active overall?

All of these things may point to the fact that jumping is painful, especially jumping down, which jolts the joints. It's only quite recently that we've realised the extent of arthritis in our older cats – largely because they've been so good at hiding it! There are diets, additives and medicines that can help arthritic cats, so don't ignore the signs. Many owners comment on how much more active their cats are after arthritis treatment – they seem much younger and do the same things that they used to. These changes alone show owners how uncomfortable their cats probably were.

Collecting urine

There are lots of clues about a cat's health in its urine, so a sample can be very useful to a vet. The difficult part is collecting it. If your cat usually uses the great outdoors then you're going to have to keep it in with a litter tray for the day

to see what you can capture. You can buy non-absorbent cat litter (your vet will probably have some) or even washed aquarium gravel, which you can buy from a pet store. Always ensure that the litter tray is clean before you start.

Once the cat has peed, drain off the urine into a sample pot – your vet may give you a pot and a syringe to help you do this. Be careful if you use a jar of your own which has previously had something sweet in it – if you don't wash it out thoroughly it may give a reading that leaves your cat's diabetic status in question!

Blood pressure

You may not realise that you can actually take a cat's blood pressure, but in fact it can be done in a fairly similar way to that used for people. A little cuff is put around the cat's front leg and inflated and a reading is taken. It only takes a few minutes and causes no pain.

As with hypertension in people, raised blood pressure can be dangerous to feline health, so it's very important to monitor blood pressure in older cats. Ideally the cat should be checked once a year from about seven or eight years old to ensure that its blood pressure is within normal ranges. High blood pressure can be linked to heart or kidney disease, or may not have an obvious cause, but either way it can lead to blindness.

If your veterinary practice uses cat-friendly techniques they'll make sure that your cat is relaxed and calm first (cats, like us, can have raised blood pressure because of the anxiety they feel from being in a hospital or surgery – so called 'white coat syndrome'), and then will gently and quietly take the reading – there's no hurrying or forcing an anxious cat!

If your cat is found to have high blood pressure your vet will investigate the causes or any problems which may stem from it and treat these, as well as being able to give medication similar to those that are used to treat people.

Cats can suffer from high blood pressure like people.

Tooth cleaning is best started in kittenhood – it does have a huge beneficial effect.

Teeth

Not many of us look in our cat's mouths. The best veterinary advice is to get our cats used to having their teeth cleaned from kittenhood. However, I suspect that this is one of those things that isn't done very often. If you do decide to brush your cat's teeth, then use a brush and paste made for cats – the usual rules regarding not using human or dog preparations for cats apply! Paste and small toothbrushes with rounded bristles, made specifically for cat use, are available from vets.

If you want to clean your cat's teeth you must first get it used to the taste of the toothpaste. Put a little on your finger and apply it to its lips or gums. If that's acceptable you can then try putting a little on the brush and, holding the cat with your hand over its head and gently pulling back the lips to reveal the teeth on one side, carefully move the brush in a circular motion. Keep these sessions short and enjoyable and increase the time spent gradually as the cat comes to accept it – a little at a time. If it ends in a fight you'll lose the fight and the war! Indeed, it may be impossible to brush some cats' teeth and in such cases it's best to retire with all of your fingers rather than persist in the attempt.

Most of us won't look in our cat's mouths at all and even the vet might have difficulty during a routine examination, so tooth decay may be difficult to diagnose. Cats can also get problems below the gum-line that may require anaesthesia to inspect. As we've already seen, cats are masters of disguise when it comes to pain and they may be suffering quite badly from a painful mouth and get to the point of actually stopping eating before we notice. Bad breath may be a clue that all is not right, but a proper inspection by the vet is needed to find out the extent of the

problem. Dental experts tell us that almost three-quarters of cats over three years old could have tooth and gum disease, so it's something to take seriously and to ask your vet about when you have your cat checked.

Cats and poisons

We all know that cats are finicky creatures when it comes to eating things. They don't just gulp food down like a dog but sniff it and try it out carefully. So you'd think that cats becoming poisoned would be a rare occurrence. However, it does happen, though not usually because the cat has eaten something that's poisonous to it.

As has been mentioned in earlier chapters, cats are very clean creatures and spend a great deal of their time keeping their coats in tip-top condition and the soft and sensitive pads of their feet clean. The need to groom and keep clean is consequently almost compulsive for cats, and this can be their undoing when it comes to ingesting substances which they would certainly never deliberately eat.

Examples of toxic substances that they might walk through or brush against with paws or coat are antifreeze, some disinfectants, creosote and other tar-based products. Decorating materials such as petroleum distillates in solvents for paints, varnishes, wood preservatives and brush cleaners (white spirit) can all cause problems too. They irritate the cat's skin and the pads of its paws and cause inflammation and blistering. If the cat grooms them off they'll cause problems in its mouth as well. Fumes from some of these products can cause breathing difficulties too.

Antifreeze is particularly toxic – it contains ethylene glycol or methanol, which can also be found in screen-

Cats may accidentally tread in substances such as creosote, which are poisonous to them.

wash and de-icers – so be very careful to clean up spillages. Signs of poisoning include weakness, breathing difficulties, convulsions and kidney damage. Treatment is difficult, and unless immediate may not be successful. A recent spate of poisoning by antifreeze in the UK has been attributed to people putting antifreeze in the water features in their

All parts of the lily plant are poisonous to cats if ingested.

gardens to stop them freezing over – cats then drink from the pond or fountain and ingest the poison.

Another very toxic substance that can be picked up by cats in the same way is the pollen from lilies. This drops off the flower stamens when they're in a vase, and the cat will then groom the pollen off its coat or feet. Indeed, all parts of the lily plant are poisonous to cats and kittens, and indoor cats without access to other green plants may become poisoned by nibbling at the leaves. Signs to look for are vomiting, not eating and depression. The cat must be got to the vet quickly, as serious damage can be done to the kidneys.

One of the other most dangerous substances that cats can't tolerate is paracetamol. Again, it's not the cat that's voluntarily eaten a tablet. Instead it's well-meaning owners who are trying to relieve pain (and have perhaps given paracetamol to their dog without any problems) who inadvertently poison their cat. Paracetamol is highly dangerous to cats – just one tablet can cause severe illness or death. Signs of paracetamol poisoning include depression, swelling of the face and paws and vomiting. There is an antidote but it needs to be used quickly.

Cats have a very different metabolism and physiology to dogs and people, so *never* assume that you can treat a cat with a human or canine product.

This is especially true when it comes to spot-on flea treatments. As has already been explained on page 104, those for dogs contain concentrated permethrin, an insecticide used in many products that has a relatively low toxicity to most mammals – except cats. Serious problems can arise if a cat is treated with the dog product, either because owners accidentally use the dog pipette or because they think they can use a small dose of the dog treatment on their cat, not realising that it's highly toxic. Sometimes problems arise because owners comb the dog after they've treated it and then use the same comb on the cat, or the cat grooms or cuddles up with the dog after it's been treated and becomes contaminated as a result. So if you use a spot-on containing permethrin on your dog, you need to keep the cat away from it for 72 hours. The obvious lessons to learn are *never* use a dog product on a cat and *always* read the instructions carefully.

Finally in the list of products most toxic to cats are slug pellets, which contain a chemical called metaldehyde. These would not be given accidentally to a cat, but it's possible that cats might sample them or perhaps step or sit on them in the garden and then ingest the poison during grooming. Symptoms to look out for are the cat becoming unsteady on its feet, salivating, twitching or suffering from convulsions. Again, urgent treatment is needed.

What to do

If you think your cat has been poisoned you need to take it away from the source of the poison and away from other animals – you don't want another cat grooming it if it's covered in something toxic. If the problem substance is on the cat's coat, skin or pads, try to stop it grooming. You can try to remove the product from the fur or skin by washing with a mild shampoo and water. Collect a sample of the substance, or part of the plant, or information from the packaging on the product you think is responsible, and let your vet know immediately. If you phone ahead your vet may be able to get any antidote ready or make enquires from the Veterinary Poisons Information Service as to what can be done. Don't try to make the cat vomit unless you're advised to do so by your vet.

Make life happier for your elderly cat

As cats get older they're at greater risk of developing various medical problems. For example, kidney disease is common in older cats, an overactive thyroid is not uncommon, and cats may also suffer from osteoarthritis. In addition older cats may have tooth or gum problems, and should also be checked for raised blood pressure, which can cause problems such as blindness. Talk to your vet about giving your older cat a really good check-up so that any problems can be caught as early as possible while they're much easier to deal with.

As has already been mentioned, obesity seems to be a problem these days even in cats, because of the availability of high-quality food and more 'indoor' lifestyles. Young and middle-aged cats may become overweight, but older cats (probably over 14 years old) may start to lose weight instead. Weight loss can also be a sign of illness, so weighing your cat regularly can help to monitor its health.

Think about your older cat's comfort – lots of little things may make a difference:

- Is the cat flap a bit stiff and difficult to push open, or does your cat have to take a big step down outside? It might appreciate not having to struggle as it comes in and out.
- Does it need help getting up on to its favourite chair or windowsill? Provide a stool or ramp that enables it to take smaller leaps if the height is becoming a problem.
- Does it need an additional litter tray so that it has easier access to it?
- Can your older cat manage its coat and keep it clean and free from matting, or does it need a little more help? As cats get older they may not be quite so supple or able to groom properly, especially if they have a long coat, so owners may need to spend time grooming them to make them comfortable.

Older cats are very precious – they understand our lives and how they fit in – they've often lived through various relationships, house-moves, babies, toddlers and even teenagers with us. Trouble is, they can become like old slippers – very comfortable and invisible and we can take them for granted. But like all our most precious things, they're irreplaceable. Look after them with care.

Saying goodbye

One of the most difficult things we have to do for our old or ill pets is to decide when it's time to let them go. This is a time to liaise with your vet, comparing what constituted normal behaviour for your cat with its present activity and

An old cat needs reassessing to ensure we are not ignoring its needs.

condition, to try and assess its quality of life. For instance, cats are motivated to keep themselves clean and tidy, and won't like having a matted coat or not being able to use the litter tray. Your vet will be able to tell you whether he or she thinks your cat is suffering, but you obviously have to feel sure that the time is right. Follow your instincts, but also remember that you're making this decision for the cat, not for yourself. You may want longer with your most

One of the most important services we can provide for our cats is to ensure they do not suffer.

favourite pet and can't bear to think of your home without its presence, but your vet will be able to give you unemotional advice about the prognosis and will be able to give your cat a pain-free, gentle and dignified release when you feel the time is right.

You can leave your cat's body with the vet for disposal and it will be cremated with others. Alternatively you may wish to arrange for an individual cremation and have the ashes returned to you – your vet will have details of the services available. Individual cremation will be more expensive but you may wish to treat your cat's body individually and have something to remember it by. You could take the body home and bury it in the garden if you have the space to do this. It's often very comforting to choose a special plant, perhaps with a name or colour which has an association with your cat, and to plant this in memory of your friend.

If you don't have a garden, you could bury your cat in a pet cemetary where you can put a permanent marker or grave stone to mark the site.

It can be very difficult to get over the death of a pet which has been with you for a long time – some cats can live with us for a very long time, seeing us grow up or have children of our own, seeing dogs come and go and generally being an integral part of the household. That little body held a great character and home is not the same without it. Sometimes people get stuck and find it hard to move on from the death. Sometimes they feel guilty that they might have acted too soon or too late, or feel that they didn't do everything they could. This is not unusual and it can be very helpful to talk to someone who understands. The Pet Bereavement Support Service, The Blue Cross and the Society for Companion Animal Studies, among others, offer telephone and email support for anyone who's experienced the loss of a pet. See page 140 for contact details.

Do cats grieve?

This is always a difficult question. We don't really know if cats grieve, but some are certainly affected by the loss of another cat. Whether they understand what's actually happened is questionable. However, the loss of another cat that's been closely involved in most aspects of its life will mean that everything changes, and this in itself can be very disorientating.

If the cat that's left relied on the other to lead or to provide confidence in stressful situations, then it may feel insecure when left alone. Added to this, routines will change, smells will alter and, no doubt, the owner's mood and behaviour will be different too (even if they're just trying to be reassuring). Give the cat attention but try and get back into a routine – it may be a bit different to before, but just knowing what's going to happen will remove some anxiety.

Owners say that their cats often show signs of 'grief' or

changes in behaviour, such as eating less, for a couple of weeks, but usually come around and seemingly return to normal after that. Don't even consider getting another cat during this time – it will only add to the disruption. Let the cat settle first, and only then should you think about it *carefully*.

There are no guidelines to help you figure out how your surviving pet will respond to a new cat. Some take very easily to a kitten, but usually less easily to an adult cat. Others will hate anything other than their original partner. In fact the cat that's left may be very happy to be an only cat, interacting with you when you're there and probably sleeping when you're out. It may not appreciate you choosing it a new 'friend'. After all, imagine having a complete stranger move in to your home and, what's more, be expected to like them or even love them!

If you do decide to get another cat, then acknowledge that it's for you, and don't expect your surviving cat to welcome it with open arms. Choose a healthy kitten or cat and introduce it carefully. Don't rush into it with the idea that another cat will cure all your problems, and don't expect the resident to be ecstatic about it on the first day!

REPRODUCTION AND YOUR CAT

When do cats come into season?

The fecundity of the cat has been acknowledged throughout its history with man – it has in consequence been worshipped by some and persecuted as wanton by others.

Up to the age of around six months, and during the months of October to December in the northern hemisphere, the free-living domestic cat is usually in what's called anoestrus, meaning it's not in a reproductive state. As with all animals which have to survive on their own, cats will have their kittens at a time when there's food available – in the spring and summer. Therefore they switch off their reproductive cycle during the winter period when food is scarce.

This process is controlled by day-length. It switches off as the days shorten in October, and when the days begin to lengthen in January it switches on again. Light entering the eye stimulates a part of the brain called the hypothalamus which regulates and controls the cat's daily rhythms such as eating, sleeping and sexual activity. The increase in daylight hours affects the pituitary gland in the brain, which produces a hormone called FSH (follicle-stimulating hormone). This in turn stimulates the ovary to produce eggs and triggers the female hormone oestrogen that affects the female cat's behaviour in readiness for reproduction.

However, for cats this time of heat, or oestrus, isn't one long period but many short periods (each cycle is about 14 days long) that begin when day-length increases and stop when it begins to decrease (unless the cat becomes

pregnant). During these 14-day periods the cat will exhibit what could be described as 'flirtatious' behaviour, rubbing and rolling on the floor, marking, and making a plaintive yet demanding rising and falling pitch known as 'calling'. Owners who haven't previously owned a female cat sometimes think that their pet is in pain and that these behaviours are signs of illness, whereas in fact they're quite normal for a cat in search of a mate.

Of course, male cats which haven't been castrated are constantly on the search for females which might be receptive to their charms. They'll pick up the scent, sound and body language signals which the female is putting out very much earlier than owners do – by the time we humans catch on to what's going on the cats will already have mated, if they have access to each other.

Several toms may congregate around the queen, and while a tom on his own territory may be more confident of winning any fight that might break out, and thus a chance to mate with the queen, she may have her own preferences. She won't accept any advances from the male until she's ready. She then exhibits what's known as the lordosis position, where she puts her rump in the air and front end on the ground and waves her tail to one side. The tom grabs her by the loose skin at the back of her neck (the scruff) and they mate briefly. At the end of this the female almost seems to attack the male cat. We don't really understand this but it may have something to do with the barbs on the penis of the male which face backwards – whether these cause pain as the tom withdraws isn't known, but the action probably has a very important effect.

Unlike animals which already have an egg in situ when mating occurs, cats don't ovulate or release eggs into the fallopian tubes and into the horns of the uterus until they've mated. So in order to become fertilised, the egg must be

A female cat in season will exhibit 'flirtatious' behaviour!

released, and the stimulus is mating; indeed, it can take several matings to stimulate ovulation. The female may mate 10 to 20 times on the first day and may mate with several toms over a period of four to six days. This long period of receptiveness gives the cat a chance to ovulate and to choose the best male, one which is healthy and in his prime.

Because it takes two days for the eggs to move down the fallopian tubes and reach the uterus, and sperm survives for several days, the resultant litter may actually have several different fathers. The eggs implant in the uterus and the resulting fetuses line up in two rows in the two horns of the uterus.

If mating doesn't occur the eggs aren't released and the cycle is repeated about two weeks later, and again every two weeks thereafter until the days start to become short in about October.

How long does pregnancy last?

After the queen becomes pregnant, her body slowly changes over the next 63 days as the foetuses grow. However, there's very little outward change in the first weeks of the pregnancy, and the first sign owners may see is a pinking of the nipples, which become more visible. She'll then gradually put on weight, and as the day of birth approaches the milk glands begin to fill.

The queen's hormones also bring about changes in her

A female may mate with several toms and the kittens in the resulting litter may have different fathers.

behaviour and she'll start to look for a good nest site in which to hide her kittens. Without the protection of a human home the safety of her kittens is far less certain. In the wild the site needs to be dry and well hidden, as it will be vital to the kittens' survival. The queen may even select several nests so that she has safe alternatives should any danger threaten her original site.

Before the birth the queen cleans around the birth passage and the teats. It's thought that she lays a trail of saliva for the kittens to follow to find a teat after they're born. Each kitten is born in a sac of amniotic fluid that the mother licks and nibbles to free the kitten. She bites through the umbilical cord and eats the kitten's placenta, and using her rough tongue she cleans the kitten and stimulates it to breathe. She then encourages the kittens to suck and keeps them warm by lying on her side and encircling them. The kittens are guided by scent and warmth to her nipples, where they find colostrum, the first type of milk to be produced, which is rich in antibodies to help protect the kittens from disease in the early weeks of their lives.

The queen purrs while the kittens are sucking – the kittens aren't able to hear when they're born, so they follow the vibrations to move towards her. They have a built-in rooting or nuzzling behaviour which helps them to

How do you sex a kitten?

If you buy a kitten from a breeder you can rely on his or her expertise to tell you what sex it is. As kittens grow this process gets easier. In female cats the anus and vulva openings are close together and look like the letter 'i'. In a male cat there are small testicles under the anus and the penis is below these.

find a nipple, latch on and stimulate the milk to flow. The suckling reflex then takes over and they feed. Kittens tend to return to the same nipple to feed, perhaps to stop them squabbling and to ensure that milk continues to be produced there because there's a demand.

At birth kittens weigh about 100g (3.5oz) but this doubles in a week and triples in three weeks. Cat milk is high in protein and fat – necessary nutrition for this rapid growth. They initially feed for many hours a day and keep the milk flowing by kneading their mother's stomach with their paws (the same behaviour they may show on our laps or on a fluffy blanket when they're older).

They remain highly dependent on their mother for two to three weeks, for feeding, cleaning, defecation and warmth. By four weeks they're using litter and copying

their mother's use of the tray; at six weeks they're grooming themselves and each other and forming bonds with their siblings. By six weeks the mother is also weaning them off her milk and onto solid food, and in the wild she would be teaching them about prey and hunting so that they can become self-sufficient as soon as possible. Indeed, in the wild the mother may well be pregnant again very soon and will have to care for new kittens while the older ones fend for themselves. Fortunately cats are intelligent, good at learning by observation, learn rapidly through play and have fantastic hunting abilities – all of which are essential in order to be able to stand on their own four feet as soon as possible.

At birth kittens are helpless, but within six weeks
are being weaned and taught about hunting.

CAT SERVICES AND PRODUCTS

Choosing a vet and making the visit less stressful

No cat owner I know relishes a trip to the vet with their cat. First of all you have to get it into the cat carrier, and it either disappears down the garden and isn't seen again for a whole day, or you get scratched in the process as the cat desperately tries to avoid being put in. Then you have to get the cat out at the veterinary surgery and hope it doesn't do the vet any damage, while at the same time you try to reassure the cat that no harm will come to it. Cats really don't like the out-of-control feeling of being off-territory, and being restrained or handled is also frightening. Though there are things that can be done to make the whole experience less stressful (see below), it's understandable that most cat owners (and cats) want to go through it as infrequently as possible.

However, if you choose the right veterinary practice these stresses can be reduced considerably. In my day job at the Feline Advisory Bureau we introduced a concept called 'Cat Friendly Practice' into veterinary treatment a couple of years ago. It was based on the expertise and experience of vets funded by the charity to specialise in cat medicine at university, who see cats on referral from vets in practice. They consequently tend to see very difficult cases that usually call for quite a lot of tests, which means in turn that the cats need to be handled and examined quite closely. These things are all a challenge, but the vets follow a particular pattern in dealing with their patients: they've learned not only how to handle cats in the least threatening way, but have also developed methods of getting them to relax more in a veterinary environment. By having a feel for cats and how they behave, they and other vets and behaviourists have been able to feed information into the FAB project to help practices in general make the whole veterinary experience less stressful. Many practices say that as a consequence they now have to deal with far fewer aggressive cats, and that the whole ethos of the practice changed once they began to 'think cat'.

You may think that vets should already have been doing this, but most have evolved from large or mixed animal practices into being small animal practices, and the working environment and ethos stem from a time when the dog was the most important small animal that they saw. Cats weren't taken seriously and practices certainly weren't designed around their needs, because nobody really thought about them. Now, however, many practices are adapting their approach and the areas in which they work to suit cats better. There are even a few cat-only practices around.

Let's take a trip to the vet in its logical order, starting with the cat basket and car journey. We'll be going to a

Taking your cat to a vets which has thought about feline welfare can make a visit much less stressful.

cat-friendly veterinary practice so that you can see what you'd hope to find in a practice that will be treating your cat – bearing in mind, as you look around, that your assessment should be based on the practice's attitude to cats rather than its specific or expensive equipment.

Right, the basket. Indeed, even before you get out the basket think about what sort of carrier you've got and how difficult it might be to use. The easiest way to get a cat in and out of a basket is through a wide opening at the top – the cat can simply be lifted in, and at the vet's lifted out. Compare this to the traditional wicker basket with a grille which swings open at one end. This can be difficult to 'stuff' the cat into, as there are lots of things to grab at on the way through the narrow opening, and even more for the cat to hold on to once it's inside and someone's trying to drag it out or tip it out on to the examination table. So there's usually a tussle to actually extract the cat, and by the time it's actually on the table everyone is stressed already, and the cat knows for certain that something dreadful is going to happen. A top-opening basket therefore seems to be the best solution to this problem. Some baskets allow for both top- and end-opening and that's fine, but avoid the ones with just an end door.

What do you do with the basket when the cat's not travelling in it? Probably, like most people, you put it away in the cupboard under the stairs or in the attic or the shed, and it only comes out when travel is imminent. It therefore smells funny, and the cat's only association with it is its last outing to the vet or cattery. No wonder the cat disappears as soon as you step off the attic ladder with the basket in your hand.

Why not make the basket part of the cat's furniture? Have it as a little den somewhere in the house where the cat might just like to curl up now and again, especially if it's near a radiator or on a windowsill (albeit a broad one) where the cat can see out of the window while feeling secure and snug. Have warm cosy things inside and perhaps drape a blanket over the top to make it part of the room. The whole thing will then smell familiar and reassuring. That way the first cause of stress is removed – the cat will consider its basket familiar territory and hopefully won't have to be forced into it in the first place. Yes, it does mean that the basket is around the house and may be in the way and perhaps won't look terribly pretty, but it does make a huge difference and there aren't many cats that can resist investigating a warm dark place with soft furnishings.

When you put the cat in to go to the vet, or anywhere else, make sure that the bedding is familiar too – don't remove it and put in fresh just because you're going out and don't want the vet or other people to see the hairs on

the blanket! Try to carry the basket without banging it on your leg. Admittedly it's quite difficult to do this because of the angle at which you have to carry it, and if you have a large, heavy cat it's somewhat taxing on the arm and difficult not to jolt it. But it just makes for a smoother journey and less upset for your cat.

Prepare the car, and the basket if it's not familiar to your cat, by spraying with an artificial pheromone (available from the vet), which will help the cat to relax. Such sprays are based on the pheromones the cat itself produces and places around your house by rubbing against the furniture to help it feel secure. Secure the basket so that it doesn't slip around or fall off the seat. You can use a seat belt or put the basket in the foot-well or secure it in the back of a hatchback. Then cover it with a blanket (as long as the weather isn't stiflingly hot, since it will remove any ventilation). This will help the cat feel even more secure.

Drive carefully, to avoid throwing the cat around inside its basket, and don't have the stereo on at full blast if the cat isn't used to loud noises. Talk reassuringly and calmly to the cat.

A top opening basket makes getting cats in and out much less of a struggle.

Now for the cat-friendly veterinary practice itself. Many practices now have a separate waiting area for cats where there are no dogs around to bark, pant or scrabble their claws on the floor, or, worst of all, to poke their noses into the basket to investigate the cat. Often there will be shelves or chairs on which you can put the cat basket so that the cat is raised off the floor – cats feel much more secure when they're viewing the world from a higher perspective. There may even be a pile of towels to use over cat baskets in order to help their occupants to relax.

Other practices may not have the space to do all of this and may instead try to provide a similar service by having cat-only clinic times or by bringing cats in directly rather than keeping them waiting in a dog-filled waiting room. They may also have signs up asking dog owners not to let their dogs sniff cats in baskets.

If you experience any of these things you're already in a practice which is 'thinking cat' and which has a positive feline attitude. You may not see much else at 'front of house' except information on notice boards that can be seen as pro-cat. Much of the rest of your visit won't require specific 'things' for your cat, but rather a way of behaving towards it that will make a great deal of difference to how it behaves itself. The practice may well use feline

pheromones to help make cats feel relaxed (though you won't notice them at all). In addition the examining room shouldn't smell of disinfectant or pine or anything else that's overly strong to a cat's sensitive nose. It will certainly smell strange, but perhaps not overwhelming. The examining table will have been wiped to ensure that the scent of the previous dog or cat has been removed.

The vet will want to examine the cat but may first simply open the door or hatch of the basket and talk to you, getting details and background, to see if the cat will come out by itself. He or she may actually be able to do some of the examination while the cat is still in its basket (if the basket allows that). Sometimes the cat is happy to keep its head under something while some gentle examination is undertaken, but at other times it will have to be taken out slowly and gently. If its bedding has to be lifted out with the cat in it and the cat be left in the bedding for a moment on the table to help it feel secure, then that's fine too.

Good cat handlers adopt the 'less is more' approach with cats. Being animals that take flight to avoid danger, they often panic if they're restrained very firmly and realise that this exit route isn't available. Even if they don't need to run off, they'll still feel the need escape from restraint – just in case. So the art of cat examination is to do the minimum,

Left: Does your vet practice 'think cat'?

Below: A gentle, less-is-more approach can pay dividends when handling cats.

Opposite: A good cattery is clean, pleasant and safe. (Courtesy of FAB Listed Cress Green Cattery, Glos.)

to get as much done as you can, confidently and gently, without too much restraint, and to leave anything too invasive until the end. The vet has only a small window of opportunity and needs to make the most of it. Some vets do a lot of the examination with the cat facing away from them, so that it's not stressed by seeing a stranger staring at it from the front. Some vets even use a windowsill so that the cat can look outside while they do most of the examination, and some let the cat wander around the room to investigate it and relax, rather than immediately pinning it down to be examined.

There may be a rubber mat on the table so that the cat doesn't feel insecure on a slippery surface, or the vet may place the cat's blanket or towel on the table for it to stand on.

I would argue that in order to treat a cat medically you need to understand the whole cat. The health of cats can be affected by stress and the results of some veterinary tests can also be affected by the changes stress can cause in the body. So understanding how a cat reacts to the world is important, and once people start to think this way many other things fall into place and it's impossible to go back to 'cat ignorance'. If the practice has a positive attitude to cats it will be because everyone has bought into the cat ethos and lots of little things have been done to make the cat's visit much more relaxing.

Many of the other things which make a veterinary practice cat friendly will be going on behind the scenes, such as having a hospitalisation ward just for cats (no barking dogs, so the environment is calm and quiet), and cages furnished to make cats feel secure and comfortable (with somewhere to hide in the cage, and something warm and cosy to lie on) so that they feel relaxed and start to eat. Eating is a great sign that a cat is feeling better and has the right attitude to helping itself to recover. Such simple things as making sure the cat has somewhere to hide, maintaining quiet in the ward and presenting food in a way that won't put it off eating can pay huge dividends in a cat's recovery.

Choosing a cattery for your cat

Some people don't go away on holiday because they don't want to leave their cat in a cattery. If the cattery in question is of poor quality then that may well be a wise decision for the cat's health and welfare. However, there are many

excellent catteries where cats are kept safe and happy and may even enjoy the experience. A holiday is sometimes necessary for human health and welfare, so understanding what a good cattery should offer and then finding one locally should leave owners free to go away with a clear conscience knowing that they'll come home to a happy cat.

Most of us have never really thought about what a cattery should look like or what services it should provide – aside from ensuring the cat can't escape and feeding it. However, the charity the Feline Advisory Bureau has been setting and improving the standard of catteries for many years and has figured it all out for us. Once you've read this section you'll never look at a cattery in the same way again, and you'll certainly never hand your cat over to one without having a good look around and asking some relevant questions.

What do you expect from a cattery?

You want to be sure your cat won't escape. It sounds very basic, but you expect your cat to be at the cattery when your return from your holiday or trip. So it needs to be escape-proof. This is achieved by ensuring that the individual cat units are built to be secure, and are properly maintained so that there are no holes or gaps through which a cat can squeeze. However, probably the easiest way to lose a cat is by letting it slip past you when you open the door to its unit – and cats are pretty good at being quick and slippery! So what you need is a type of safety corridor, like an airlock in a spaceship. The outside door is always kept shut when the inside one is opened and vice versa. Good catteries will therefore have an area outside the cat units that's secure, so that if a cat slips out of its own space it's still safe inside the cattery. Trained staff who understand the importance of door-shutting are equally important, as the only way a cat can escape from this set-up is by human error – and this should be an exceptionally rare occurrence in any well-run cattery.

Next you want to be sure that your cat will be warm and comfortable. There are different types of cattery out there – some are totally indoors, some have units like little chalets that also have an outdoor run, and some are sort of in-between. You might instinctively think you want your cat to stay indoors, but it can be much more rewarding and healthier for them to have an outdoor run (with a roof and safely fenced to prevent escape) which is in the fresh air. Inside the little unit there should be a cosy bed, and a heater in case it gets cold. Of course, the heater has to be safe – either a radiator type or what's called an infrared bulb, which heats the air around it (you may have seen these being used with orphan lambs or other small creatures which need to be kept warm). A cat flap will let the cat in and out of the chalet or unit so that it can choose where it wants to be. The flap needs to be shut at night to keep the cat indoors.

And then there are things that you probably don't even think about, because they don't enter your everyday

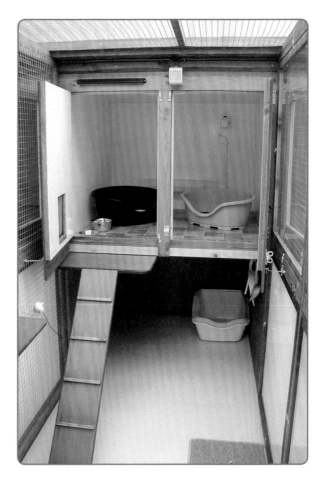

An example of penthouse cattery accommodation which opens into a secure run.

thinking about your cat. You just want him to have a cosy place to stay without fear of escape, but there's a lot more to it than that. There are some nasty viruses that affect cats and they love to hop from cat to cat given the opportunity. They do this via grooming, via droplets from sneezes, through bites, through contact with faeces, from shared food-bowls, or even from the clothes of people who've touched cats that are excreting viruses. If you have several cats that live together they've shared each other's bacteria and viruses. However, if cats are brought together in a cattery, the latter must do its utmost to ensure that they don't catch anything from other cats that they're looking after. This is where the design and management of the cattery come into effect. Cats from different households should never be able to touch each other, and they should be protected from the danger of another cat sneezing on them or from transmitting disease on the hands or clothes of cattery carers or on food-bowls or litter trays. So the design of the cattery is important – the individual cat units can be alongside each other, but they need to be separated either by an impermeable barrier such as Perspex or by a wide gap, often referred to as a 'sneeze barrier' as that's its

An example of a full-height chalet which opens into a secure run.

While the design of a cattery is obviously very important to both prevention of escape and prevention of the spread of disease, the management of the cattery is equally important. You may see notices for visitors not to touch the cats because stroking them can spread disease. Cattery proprietors themselves should wash their hands between handling cats, and many now use hand-washes like the ones hospital staff use to prevent the spread of infection and MRSA.

For most of us our cats are important members of the family and we want them to be looked after with the same care and consideration that we give them. That's down to the people caring for the cats and the enthusiasm and dedication they give to the job. If you look at the very best catteries you'll recognise that the people involved love cats and each one is important to them. There's attention to detail and knowledge behind that care which comes from their love of cats.

I've spoken to owners who haven't had a holiday for years because they feel their cat won't survive without them – that it will probably pine and won't eat. If you talk to cattery proprietors you'll find that most cats settle down very well and very happily. If they don't, a good cattery and proprietor will ensure that they nurture the cats and help them to settle in. Indeed, most cats actually adapt very quickly and as long as they feel secure in their new environment and they have food, warmth and toilet facilities they make the best of the cosiness and the run to sleep and watch everything going on in the cattery's daily routine. And as I've said before, routine makes them feel secure – they know when they're going to be fed, they see when people come and go and they don't feel threatened.

Almost every parent will have faced the trauma of leaving a screaming child at a nursery school and having to go away feeling absolutely terrible. Of course, the nursery staff know that as soon as the parent is out of the door the child is absolutely fine and joins in quite happily with the school routine. And it's much the same with cats. Of course, cats are much less likely to be bonded so strongly to their 'parents' anyway, so thinking that your cat won't cope may be an excuse not to leave home, but it won't necessarily be for the sake of the cat.

Good cattery proprietors will find out about your cat's favourite food, whether it needs grooming, and what its little foibles are – these are all important in helping the cat to fit in. They'll try to feed it the same food as at home and will let owners bring in familiar bedding or toys to help the cat feel secure. Most catteries will give medication if it's required and a few of the best will even give treatment such as insulin injections for diabetic cats. Obviously, if you have a higher maintenance cat that needs such medication you need to search out a cattery that's capable of providing the required treatment.

Good proprietors will monitor your cat – they'll even have what's called a 'pee and poo' chart which records what happens in the litter tray, as well as noting what the

function. Cats should never be able to touch each other through the mesh.

Some catteries offer communal areas where cats share a large space with other cats (not from the same household). Many owners naively think this will be lovely – the cat will have 'friends' and it will be able to run around and play with them. However, if you've read the opening chapters of this manual you'll know by now that many cats don't want to share space with a cat they don't know and will be very stressed by this. In addition such communal spaces enable cats to share litter trays, lick each other and share food-bowls – all potential ways to spread disease.

Likewise if the cattery says that their cats go out into a communal area to exercise and then back into their individual pens, avoid it like the plague – this is a potential virus-sharing scenario too. Cats should be in individual runs that are kept meticulously clean and should never come into contact with cats from another household. If the cattery is well built and the runs are about 6ft by 4ft (1.8m by 1.2m), with shelves to sunbathe on, and the run is equipped with something for cats to sharpen their claws on, they'll be very content.

cat is eating. This gives them a very good idea of the cat's wellbeing, as well as enabling them to notice if it has an upset stomach and so on. Any cat that's unwell will be taken to the vet – and again, a good cattery will ask you for details of your own vet as well as asking you to sign a consent form allowing them to contact a vet and give treatment if it's necessary. Vaccinations are vital for a cat coming into a cattery because of the presence of lots of cats and therefore viruses, and a cattery must ask to see the cat's vaccination certificate as proof that its inoculations are up to date, in order to protect both your cat and the other cats in the cattery.

If you want to find a good cattery you should visit the Feline Advisory Bureau website. The charity has a Listing Scheme for catteries in which they help with design and management information and then go along and inspect the cattery to ensure that it attains a high standard of care. Have a look on the FAB website at www.fabcats.org, which includes pictures of some fantastic catteries – around 200 across the UK with a few in Ireland. Once you've seen these you'll have a much better idea of what to look for in your own area. If you can't find anything of good quality (there are some very poor catteries out there, even though they should have been inspected by the local authority to get a licence to operate), then you may want to look a little further afield. Even if your cat doesn't really like travelling in the car an extra half-hour (it won't harm the cat even if it doesn't really enjoy it), it may well be worth it for peace of mind while you're away.

If you go to look around a cattery and the proprietor won't let you see where the cats are kept then go elsewhere – a good proprietor will have nothing to hide and will be proud to show you their cattery.

Choosing insurance

We all know it makes sense – insuring your cat so that if it becomes ill or comes off worst in an argument with another cat, dog or car we can simply say to the vet 'do whatever you need to do', knowing that the treatment is covered by insurance. But of course, it's another regular cost in the monthly accounts, and if you don't use it you may feel it's a complete waste of money. However, if something does happen it can come into its own – like all insurances. Pet insurance is actually the most claimed general insurance policy, more even than household or motor insurances, and over 95 per cent of pet insurance claims are for veterinary fees, so this is the aspect you need to concentrate on. Be aware that most insurance policies don't cover regular preventive care such as vaccination, worming, flea treatment or neutering.

 For cats there are times of their lives when there's more risk of accident or illness than at others. Kittens and young

cats are curious, can be very unwise near traffic and can just get themselves into scrapes, so it really makes sense to insure your kitten immediately you get it. Indeed, if you buy a pedigree cat or if you get it from some rescue organisations it will come with about six weeks' free insurance in order to cover that transition period. This is sensible, as it can be stressful to change homes and this can affect a cat's immunity and make it susceptible to infectious diseases.

A cat's first year is probably its most hazardous, so insurance is a wise move. After this there may be periods in its life – when it's between perhaps three and nine years old – when your cat is really healthy and hearty and you wonder why you're paying out for insurance. However, once the cat becomes a bit more mature there are illnesses that may affect it, and if it's lucky enough to live into its teens problems like kidney disease become common. Many insurers also have an age beyond which they won't take your pet on as a new client, most often around 8–10. Therefore you need to make sure you insure your cat before it reaches the cut-off age.

Many of the problems that affect older cats need long-term treatment, so if you're thinking about taking out insurance you need to read the small print very carefully. This is because some insurances will only cover a particular problem for a year and then, on renewal the next year, will exclude that particular illness. Of course, if you then want to get another insurance this becomes a pre-existing problem and so won't be covered by that policy either. You may therefore want to opt for an insurance providing lifetime cover – *ie* one which will cover any particular illness for life. It will give your cat a fixed amount of insurance cover each year for veterinary fees and will cover treatment for the cat's life. This is obviously the most expensive sort of insurance but it may well save you money in the long run. About a third of claims on lifetime insurances are for conditions which last for over 12 months.

Other insurances have a maximum cover and will pay out up to that amount, or will cover a certain condition for up to a fixed amount. Alternatively you might buy a 12-month policy that gives your cat a fixed amount of cover for a condition over a fixed period of time. However, previous conditions wouldn't be covered the following year. Other things which may be covered in a pet insurance policy include loss of your pet, and cattery fees should you need to go into hospital.

There are hundreds of pet insurances available, from supermarkets to specialist pet insurers. Decide what you want and read the conditions carefully so that you're not disappointed when you actually come to need it. Check the excess – the amount you'll be expected to pay if you actually make a claim. This can be a flat rate or a percentage of the claim or a mixture of the two. Speak to a range of insurers to get a feel for the quality of their customer service.

All insurers are covered by the Financial Services Act and have to abide by its rules.

Toys

In some ways cats are like children – they know how to manipulate us, they teach us to fetch and carry for them, they want us to play with them, and they prefer the box and the wrapping to the present which came in it! So toys for cats need not be expensive or elaborate. The most important thing is that they move – and that requires owner input!

In a survey FAB carried out a few years ago 40 per cent of respondents said that their cat retrieved. While you might expect this response from a survey on dogs, it's surprising for cats. Further investigation revealed that many of these cats were quite young or had started this interaction with their owners when they were young. Some were pedigree breeds such as Burmese or Siamese, which often initiate more interaction than their moggie counterparts and could be said to be a bit more 'dog-like' in their behaviour. Some didn't have access to the outside and so had lots of energy and enjoyed the stimulation.

When you watch cats playing this way you realise where the training is happening – the cat is actually training its owner to join in and to throw the toy, then bringing it back to start again, rather than the other way around. Carrying prey is a natural behaviour for cats and they'll bring it back to a place of safety to eat it or will carry it back for their kittens, so fetching is just an extension of what comes naturally anyway. The unusual part is the vigour with which these cats encourage the interaction with their owners and enjoy the game. As they get older this often slows down a little. However, if you have an indoor cat or one that prefers not to go out

because it's nervous, then a game of fetch, especially up and down the stairs, is great exercise for the cat and great bonding for owners and pets alike.

Cats love simple toys such as balls of paper, ping-pong balls, tents of newspaper and cardboard boxes – all cheap and cheerful. They also enjoy those toys which look a bit like fishing rods with a feather or little item on the end of a string or wire which can be made to move quickly and jerkily as you 'fish' the cat with it. Keep some of their toys stored away so that they maintain a degree of novelty.

Of course, with movement being the key to success owner input is greatly appreciated. It's a great way to provide exercise and to help cats get rid of those beans they're sometimes so full of! But always use toys rather than your hands, as kittens may otherwise get used to grabbing, scratching and biting hands, and while this may be fine when they're little, when their weapons become larger and the cat stronger they can cause damage and certainly pain. Children can be frightened by cats that do

this and haven't learned to be gentle or to hold back in play, or even annoyance. So controlled play avoiding contests of physical strength are best.

Catnip

A plant that we call catnip (its proper name is *Nepeta cataria*) has an extraordinary effect on around 80 per cent of cats. An encounter with either the plant itself or with a catnip-stuffed toy causes them to become excited, and they sniff and roll on it. The active chemical in the plant is called nepetalactone and has been likened to LSD. However, its effect is short-lived and harmless – just a little drug trip that cats seem to enjoy.

Often a single catnip plant in the garden will have barely sprouted out of the ground before the cat starts to roll all over it, and cat-owning gardeners will have to grow lots of these plants in order that one plant doesn't get too much of a 'cat hit' and never actually get to grow! Another way to help the plant get some shoots out of the ground is to cover it with an upturned hanging basket or something similar until it's established itself.

A cat that's affected by this plant (it's genetically controlled whether cats react or not, and kittens aren't affected – why will become clear further on) will often exhibit that very interesting cat behaviour, the flehmen response, for which see page 16. Of course, this mechanism isn't just there just to get a bigger 'hit' from this interesting plant, it's to assist in reproduction and feeding, but cats will exhibit the flehmen 'grin' whenever they sample air inside their mouth. On the outside it looks like the cat's grinning or even grimacing as it opens its mouth and draws the air in to sample it. This usually happens when it's sniffing the urine of a cat that's in season or where a tom has sprayed. It gives cats a great deal of information about the scent and the cat that laid it. This is probably the reason why kittens don't react to catnip, which obviously stimulates similar pathways in the brain and often makes the cat act as it does when it's in season, rolling around and being what we might call flirtatious. The reaction to catnip therefore probably begins when a cat becomes sexually mature at around six months.

Catnip can be used to help introduce cats to one another, either as a distraction or to help them to relax – definitely worth a try. A cat won't play unless it feels relaxed enough, so a catnip toy could encourage this behaviour too.

Scratch posts

In the garden cats will use trees and wooden fence posts to help them to pull off the old covering to their claws to reveal fresh sharp new points. These scratch posts also act as physical and scent markers for the cat. If you have an indoor cat it will use furniture or carpet to undertake this behaviour. So you must provide an outlet for this natural behaviour and a way for your cat to keep its claws in tip top condition if you don't want it to ruin your home. Even some cats with access to the outdoors also scratch indoors, so a scratch post may be useful indoors too.

Scratch posts come in all shapes, sizes and materials, from sisal wrapped poles to chunks of compressed paper, or wood. You could also provide your cat with a bark covered post or a large branch which it could scratch as if it was outside; you can use a post wrapped in sisal or even carpet. Whether having a carpet-covered post encourages the use of carpet elsewhere or it gives the cat an outlet for its preference for carpet is debatable. When cats scratch outside they tend to try and find tall posts where they can stretch up high and pull down and this might point to using a post which is tall but not unsteady. There are lots of different designs of cat play centres which incorporate scratch posts as well as giving the cat high resting places. It also provides a good place for exercise.

Collars and harnesses

Should my cat wear a collar?

Cats are often free to come and go from our homes without hindrance – that's the joy of being a cat. The problem is that cats do get lost and do get into trouble. If they climb into someone's van and get driven off and then handed into a rescue organisation you'll never know what happened to them if they have no identification. Likewise, if they're unlucky enough to be run over you may never know, because the person who hit them won't know whom to contact. So obviously, some means of identifying them is vital.

There are two main ways of achieving this. This first is via microchipping, where a small rice-sized glass bead is inserted under the skin. It has a unique number that can be read by machines kept by vets, rescue organisations and some local authorities. The number is logged into a database, which, as long as you keep it notified of any change of address, can let you know if your cat has been found.

However, some people prefer to put a collar on their cat with a visible address tag that will be more obvious to a finder or someone who doesn't have access to a chip reader.

There are some drawbacks to collars. The choice is very important. Cats are pretty good at getting themselves into trouble, especially the young ones, so give them something

around their neck and there's a fair chance they'll get it caught on something as they climb trees or scramble through shrubbery and so on. When such incidents first came to light it seemed a good idea to add a length of elastic to the collar, in order to allow the cat to extract itself and not become choked. However, it then became apparent that this was potentially even more dangerous, because instead of just wiggling their head out when they got into trouble they often managed to get themselves only part-way out, usually getting one front leg through so that the collar ended up sitting under what we'd call the armpit. Because by this time the elastic has been stretched to its limit the leg is trapped in such a way that even the most supple of cats can't wriggle free. Unless the collar is removed quickly it can then start to cut in under the leg and cause wounds that can be very difficult to treat and to heal because they're where the skin stretches when a cat walks.

Elastic collars and badly fitting collars (too loose) can also get caught around the jaw, or even around the cat's middle, so it's important with such an escapologist to fit

collars snugly (tight enough to get only one to two fingers underneath) and that the fit is checked carefully as the cat grows – a kitten grows rapidly and cats can also put on weight as they age, and run the risk of being choked. The best option is a 'snap open' or safety collar, which has a fixing which opens if the cat gets into trouble. Some take quite a bit of pulling to open, so check them when you buy one, but they're definitely the safest way to put a collar on a cat. Ensure too that the collar is of good quality, without bits of stitching that can come undone and get caught around the cat's teeth or mouth.

A collar should always be used to aid identification, with either an engraved disc or a tube containing your address on a slip of paper, or with the address written on the inside of the collar itself. Because they're not risk-free it's unwise to give your cat a collar merely as a fashion accessory – cats are already beautiful enough, they don't need clothes or jewellery. A reflective strip on the collar will help cats to be seen at night, as it will show up in car headlights.

Flea collars too are really a thing of the past. The collar itself adds risks to a cat's life and there are now much better alternatives that deal with fleas far more effectively.

For the problematical subject of collars fitted with bells as a means of warning off birds, see page 42.

Teaching your cat to wear a collar or harness

If you want a kitten or a cat to wear a collar or harness then it's best to start early. Choose a soft collar or harness with no bits that the animal can get itself tangled in or which might get snagged in its claws. Fit it properly and then just leave it on for a little while. Don't leave the cat unattended, particularly if it's a kitten, and distract it with play or food so that it doesn't get upset about the collar. Then take it off, and when you repeat the process do it for a little longer. If the first session wasn't too bad then the cat will react less adversely the next time. Praise it for accepting the collar and reward it with a treat if it demonstrates the behaviour you want. Gradually extend the length of the sessions and take your cue from the cat or kitten.

If you want to use a harness with a lead, so that you can take the cat out, then this too is a new experience that needs to be approached gradually. Remember that a cat is a creature of flight – its natural response to a situation it doesn't like is to remove itself as quickly as possible. If its exit is restricted by a lead it's likely to become stressed and excited and may panic, so you need to take things very slowly and let the cat get used to this restriction. The harness only needs to be light, but it must be soft and pliable. Likewise the lead can be light, since strength isn't the main requirement – controlling a cat isn't like holding on to a Rottweiler!

Attach a lightweight piece of string or cord to the harness first. Hold the end gently and allow the cat to walk a little – encourage it forward with food if you have to. If

Above: Cats can wear a harness successfully but calm, gentle introductions are required.

Below: Cats are great escape artists, so cat-proofing the garden requires planning.

the cat moves in the other direction follow it gently without restricting its movement. If it dashes away drop the cord, and try again later. Once it's become accustomed to the string, progress to a light lead. Always praise and reward the cat when it shows the relaxed behaviour you're looking. Once it's calm with you holding the lead when you're indoors you can progress to outdoors. Choose a quiet time and only venture into the garden. Do just a little bit and then go indoors again. Prevent anything going wrong and the cat will gradually gain confidence and get used to the restriction of the lead without feeling the need to panic.

Make sure *you* are in control of the lead and don't let the cat tie you in knots – keep the lead relatively short until your cat is used to it. Don't begin with a flexi-lead (one which can extend a long distance and automatically winds in at the press of a button), as these are quite heavy and you need to concentrate on the cat and not on feeding the lead in and out. The temptation is also to let a cat take this sort of lead out to its full length, the trouble then being that if it panics and runs the lead may well get caught in or around something, which will make the cat panic even more. It's therefore best to start with a very simple lead which is at most 2m long. Once the cat is relaxed and happy with the harness and the concept of being unable to run away, *then* you can try the flexi-lead so that it can wander more freely.

Fencing-in your garden

Some people don't get a cat because they don't feel it's fair to keep it permanently indoors but fear that it'll be run over or injured because they live near a busy road or an area that could be dangerous for cats. However, the problem of keeping an active cat in a safe environment can be solved without necessarily condemning the cat to a life indoors.

There are two ways of doing this. The first is to fence in the garden, either completely or in part, to prevent the cat from getting out. The second is to build a run.

Escape can be prevented by putting up high fencing with an overhang that stops cats from simply climbing over it. Of course, gardens all vary in size and complexity and most will have some sort of obstacle that might be difficult to accommodate. Perimeter trees can be a problem, as a cat could simply climb these and jump over the fence. Such problems as uneven ground and overhanging branches will also need to be solved.

A fence to confine a cat needs to be at least 1.8m (6ft) high. It can be rigid or flexible depending on the type of wiring or netting you use. The actual escape-prevention system needs to be constructed at the top. There are various methods of doing this, using either a fixed framework or brackets and stretcher wires. It can comprise a horizontal

Above and below: One method of securing the garden is to attach poles along the top of all boundaries, such as these versions from Katzecure.

section, jutting out at right angles into the garden for at least 0.5m (18in–2ft), or it can be built at an upward angle of 45°.

Either way an overhang is created, but the 45° angle may be less attractive to jump on to if the cat has access to trees that enable it to get above the fence height.

The wire also needs to be buried in the ground so that the cat can't pull it out and escape and so that other animals can't break in. The overhang can also be developed into a 'T' shape or a 'Y' shape, rather than simply an upside

A purpose-built enclosure is an alternative if your garden is not suitable for fencing in.

down 'L' shape, so as to prevent outside cats from getting into the garden.

Any gates giving access to the garden will have to be given similar treatment, and any gaps underneath them will need to be dealt with. A 'please shut the gate' notice may also help here.

The use of trellis sections can improve the appearance of safety fencing and will permit lightweight trailing plants to be trained along it.

Fencing the trees themselves is a possibility by means of 'bonneting', or giving the tree an Elizabethan-style collar. Branches that pose a problem can be trimmed, but check first if you live in a designated conservation area or if any trees in your garden are subject to a Tree Preservation Order. If so you must consult the planning department of your local council before trimming or pruning.

It's always wise to discuss plans for a new fence or garden wall with neighbours to ensure that no objections will occur. Large fences may need planning consent from the local council, so it's important to check before you commence construction.

If your garden isn't suitable for fencing-in, an alternative solution is to create a purpose-built enclosure specifically for your cat. If it can be accessed from the house and has a roof it can be used throughout the year and the cat can

come and go as it pleases. It may be open, in the sense that its 'walls' are constructed with the same type of fence and overhang as described previously for the whole garden, or it may be totally enclosed with a roof, made either of wire mesh, like a fruit cage, or of PVC. Once again, it's advisable to consult the local planning department to check on any regulations with regard to such structures. If the run is separate from the house you may want to put in some type of small accommodation unit, somewhat like those used in catteries, where the cat can shelter if the weather changes and you're not available to let it in immediately.

Similarly, the question of access to food, bedding and possibly litter trays arises. If access between the house and the outside run is open 24 hours a day there should be no problem. Cats that are used to being shut in at night may, in poor weather, still prefer to use the litter tray rather than go out into the rain. Clean drinking water must be available at all times, so if access to the house is limited extra provision must be made for this.

Whatever type of enclosure is created, it's important to provide play areas for the cats. If the garden doesn't already offer such amusement facilities, then the provision of scratching posts, shelves and climbing frames made from branches may prevent your cat from giving too much thought to the possibility of escape.

If you'd like more details on the construction of cat enclosures, or on companies which might undertake the work for you or be able to offer alternative systems, visit the Feline Advisory Bureau website at www.fabcats.org.

USEFUL CONTACTS

Association of Pet Behaviour Counsellors

The APBC is an international network of experienced and qualified pet behaviour counsellors, who, on referral from veterinary surgeons, treat behaviour problems in dogs, cats, birds, rabbits, horses and other pets.
PO Box 46
Worcester WR8 9YS England
tel 01386 751151 *fax* 01386 750743
email info@apbc.org.uk
website www.apbc.org.uk

Cats Protection

Formed in 1927, Cats Protection rehomes and reunite 55,500 cats and kittens every year, through its network of over 250 volunteer-run branches and 29 adoption centres.
National Cat Centre, Chelwood Gate, Haywards Heath
Sussex RH17 7TT
tel (Switchboard) 08707 708649
(National Helpline) 08702 099099
(Adoption Centre) 08707 708650
email helpline@cats.org.uk
website www.cats.org.uk

Feline Advisory Bureau

FAB is a cat charity that provides information on cat care, disease, treatment, behaviour and all other things feline to improve the health and welfare of the cat. There is a wealth of information on its website.
Feline Advisory Bureau
Taeselbury
High Street, Tisbury
Wiltshire SP3 6LD
tel 01747 871872
website www.fabcats.org

Governing Council of the Cat Fancy

The GCCF is the primary governing body of the Cat Fancy in the United Kingdom, the feline equivalent of the Kennel Club.
Governing Council of the Cat Fancy
5 King's Castle Business Park
The Drove
Bridgwater
Somerset TA6 4AG
tel 01278 427575
website www.gccfcats.org

Pet Food Manufacturers' Association

PFMA is the principal trade association for the prepared pet food industry and currently comprises 55 member companies. Collectively, its members represent about 90 per cent of the UK market and produce a whole range of products for cats, dogs and other pet animals.
The Pet Food Manufacturers' Association
20 Bedford Street, London WC2E 9HP
tel 020 7379 9009
email info@pfma.org.uk

Society for Companion Animal Studies

The SCAS is a charity dedicated to understanding how interactions between people and companion animals can improve quality of life and well-being. It also runs the Pet Bereavement Support Service in conjunction with The Blue Cross animal welfare charity.
SCAS, The Blue Cross, Shilton Road, Burford
Oxon OX18 4PF
tel 01993 825597   *fax* 01993 825598
website www.scas.org.uk

RSPCA

The RSPCA's vision is to work for a world in which all humans respect and live in harmony with all other members of the animal kingdom. The RSPCA will, by all lawful means, prevent cruelty, promote kindness to and alleviate suffering of animals.

RSPCA Enquiries Service, Wilberforce Way, Southwater, Horsham, West Sussex RH13 9RS.
www.rspca.org.uk

BATTERSEA

Battersea Dogs and Cats Home, as the title suggests, deals with cats as well as dogs, and indeed often deals with more cats than dogs. The charity reunites lost dogs and cats with their owners; when it can't do this, it cares for them until new homes can be found for them. Every year the Home takes in around 12,000 dogs and cats.
www.battersea.org.uk